"Isaac the Syrian, who lived in the seventh century, is a writer who has the remarkable gift of being able to speak directly and relevantly over the centuries. In this splendidly imaginative presentation, Dr. Andrew Mayes offers an excellent guided tour to different aspects of his teaching on the spiritual life."

—Sebastian Brock, Oriental Institute, Oxford University

"This book began with the author's teaching in Bahrain, where for centuries the country's economy was based on pearl fishing. Isaac's pearling imagery resonates with us in our modern and postmodern world with wisdom, freshness, and depth. Canon Andrew Mayes makes the writings of this Gulf saint beautifully accessible for the wider contemporary Church, both for individual reflection and for group study."

—Christopher Butt, formerly dean, St. Christopher's Cathedral Bahrain

"The treasures to be found in these pages are many. Andrew's deep, thought-provoking 'questions for reflection' and imaginative 'prayer exercises' are suitable for individual readers, an excellent resource for spiritual directors, and helpful for supervision. For retreat leaders there is the gift of outlines for use of this material in quiet day and retreat settings. Dive away!"

—Maggie Le-Roy, retreats facilitator, Anglican Diocese of Cyprus and the Gulf

"I was introduced to the works of Isaac the Syrian by Dr. Mayes and this material, and it led me into a deeper experience of prayer and of God than I had ever known before. I come back to *exploring* and *resting* in the ocean depths of God time and again, and am enlivened every time I apply Isaac's insights to my prayers. This book invites constant study, and constant application—I am immeasurably richer for it."

—Revd. Roy Shaw, bishop's external spiritual director for the Archdeaconry of Cyprus

MONASTIC WISDOM SERIES: NUMBER SIXTY-THREE

Diving for Pearls

Exploring the Depths of Prayer with Isaac the Syrian

Andrew D. Mayes

α

Cistercian Publications
www.cistercianpublications.org

LITURGICAL PRESS
Collegeville, Minnesota
www.litpress.org

A Cistercian Publications title published by Liturgical Press

Cistercian Publications
Editorial Offices
161 Grosvenor Street
Athens, Ohio 45701
www.cistercianpublications.org

Unless otherwise noted, Scripture quotations are from New Revised Standard Version Bible © 1989 National Council of the Churches of Christ in the United States of America. Used by permission. All rights reserved worldwide.

Scripture quotations marked (RSV) are from the Revised Standard Version of the Bible, copyright © 1946, 1952, and 1971 National Council of the Churches of Christ in the United States of America. Used by permission. All rights reserved worldwide.

Scripture quotations marked (*The Message*) copyright © by Eugene H. Peterson 1993, 1994, 1995, 1996, 2000, 2001, 2002. Used by permission of NavPress. All rights reserved. Represented by Tyndale House Publishers, Inc.

Scripture quotations marked (*The Voice*) taken from The Voice™. Copyright © 2008 by Ecclesia Bible Society. Used by permission. All rights reserved.

Scripture quotations marked (*The Passion Translation*®) copyright © 2017, 2018, 2020 by Passion & Fire Ministries, Inc. Used by permission. All rights reserved. www.thepassiontranslation.com.

Scripture quotations marked (*The Living Bible*) copyright © 1971 by Tyndale House Foundation. Used by permission of Tyndale House Publishers Inc., Carol Stream, Illinois 60188. All rights reserved.

Scripture quotations marked (NASB) are from New American Standard Bible®, Copyright © 1960, 1971, 1977, 1995, 2020 by the Lockman Foundation. All rights reserved.

Excerpts from *Isaac of Nineveh: The Second Part, Chapters IV–XLI*. Trans. Sebastian Brock. Leuven: Peeters, 1995. Used by permission.

Excerpts from *Isaac the Syrian's Spiritual Works*. Trans. Mary T. Hansbury. Piscataway, NJ: Gorgias Press, 2016. Used with permission.

1   2   3   4   5   6   7   8   9

Library of Congress Cataloging-in-Publication Data

Names: Mayes, Andrew D., author.
Title: Diving for pearls : exploring the depths of prayer with Isaac the Syrian / Andrew D. Mayes.
Description: Collegeville, Minnesota : Cistercian Publications/Liturgical Press, [2021] | Series: Monastic wisdom series ; Number sixty-three | Includes bibliographical references. | Summary: "Diving for Pearls is a prayer resource based on the writings of seventh-century Isaac the Syrian. It includes questions for individual or group reflection at the end of every chapter and a range of prayer exercises"— Provided by publisher.
Identifiers: LCCN 2021008995 (print) | LCCN 2021008996 (ebook) | ISBN 9780879071639 (paperback) | ISBN 9780879075637 (epub) | ISBN 9780879075637 (mobi) | ISBN 9780879075637 (pdf)
Subjects: LCSH: Prayer—Christianity. | Spiritual life—Christianity. | Isaac, Bishop of Nineveh, active 7th century.
Classification: LCC BV215 .M3723 2021 (print) | LCC BV215 (ebook) | DDC 248.3/2—dc23
LC record available at https://lccn.loc.gov/2021008995
LC ebook record available at https://lccn.loc.gov/2021008996

CONTENTS

Acknowledgments

I wish to place on record my gratitude, first of all, to Dr. Sebastian Brock, both for his inspirational translation of the Second Part of Isaac's corpus, and also for his encouragement and support in the preparation of this resource. In particular I am grateful to Dr. Brock for entrusting to me his personal account of his discovery of a thousand-year-old document that gives the world the Second Part of Isaac's remarkable writings. I thank the Peeters Publishers of Leuven for their gracious permission to reprint substantial extracts from the English translation.

I also pay tribute to Mary T. Hansbury (d. 2021) for her significant translations of Isaac, and I thank her publishers, Gorgias Press, Piscataway, New Jersey, for permission to use extracts from her translation of Part Three of Isaac's writings.

I thank Dr. Marsha Dutton, the executive editor of Cistercian Publications, for her unstinting assistance and advice in the editing of this book.

I am grateful to the Diocese of Cyprus and the Gulf for giving me the opportunity as its spirituality adviser to try and test meditations from this material, both on the island of Cyprus and in the cathedral of St. Christopher, Bahrain.

Andrew D. Mayes
Borderlands Retreats
Leominster, Herefordshire, United Kingdom
www.spiritualityadviser.com

PREFACE

This book invites you to a spiritual odyssey. It opens before you an itinerary for venturing forth with God. It is a handbook of the soul and a map for the journey. This practical resource brings ancient wisdom—long lost but recently rediscovered—into today's Christian spirituality and discipleship.

When I served as Spirituality Advisor to the Diocese of Cyprus and the Gulf, I led retreats and quiet days on these texts, including in Bahrain, in the very region where Isaac of Nineveh grew up and found inspiration in the natural environment around him. This gave me the opportunity to engage spiritually with texts that have hitherto received mainly scholarly attention and to explore how they resonate with our contemporary spiritual search, inspiring me to share their richness with others on the spiritual journey.

Through this resource, the seventh-century Isaac of Nineveh today invites us to become fearless and curious explorers of the spiritual life. He leads us to an ocean of grace teeming with mystery and wonder. He summons us to be expectant and ready to stumble on astonishing treasures in the depths of prayer. We fulfill Isaac's own prayer: "Grant us to search unceasingly in wonder" (3/VII:42).[1]

---

1. See the Introduction, pp. 1–13, for the list of translations of Isaac's works cited in this book, and for an explanation of the citation form in each case.

This book is a summons to a spiritual adventure. With the guidance of Isaac of Nineveh, its aim is to invigorate and inspire a search for something deeper in the spiritual life, as we progress in a journey of discovery. We will risk the depths, face the darkness, and make astonishing, transformative discoveries. This is a book for the curious, for the inquisitive—for people who sense that there is much yet to find in their spiritual quest.

Again, the kingdom of heaven is like a merchant in search of fine pearls; on finding one pearl of great value, he went and sold all that he had and bought it (Matt 13:45).

This key text becomes a seminal inspiration for Isaac of Nineveh. His imagery, drawn from the nautical world, is for us a powerful lens with which we can observe the spiritual life in greater clarity. Isaac was not a systematic writer, and approaching his texts can be an overwhelming experience, but this image of the pearl (and the ocean) provides a helpful focus and direct way into his teaching. We use the lens he offers to identify key movements and opportunities in the spiritual life.

This is a book to inspire preachers and teachers on prayer. It will stimulate and provide resources for spiritual directors and retreat-givers, and it provides material ideally suited to quiet days and retreats. But it is also for seekers, for those who want to leave the shallows and launch out into the deep in their spiritual journey.

A practical resource, it includes at the end of every chapter questions for individual or group reflection and a range of prayer exercises. It can be used as a course for a home group, or a study guide to introduce Isaac the Syrian or to introduce the concept of receptive, listening prayer. It becomes a hand book on contemplative prayer, highlighting key concepts in the mystical journey. It can be a useful element or module in spiritual-direction training. An appendix offers biblical backgrounds and ready-made outlines for retreat work.

Isaac the Syrian

Little known in the West, Isaac is one of the most loved saints of the Eastern church. Known as the Syrian, he never lived in Syria but wrote in Syriac (related to the Aramaic of Jesus' day), the language of the Church of the East.

Isaac's astonishing writings, which celebrate the all-encompassing love of God and the call to deeper prayer, have only recently been rediscovered and rendered into English. For more than a thousand years only the first volume (called the First Part) was known—translated from Syriac to Greek in the ninth century by the monks of Mar Saba, Palestine. This first volume was translated into English by Leiden Professor of Semitic Languages Arent Jan Wensinck, from Fr. Paul Bedjan's Syriac edition, and published in Amsterdam in 1923. It was known at that time that other parts of Isaac's writings must have existed, but they were feared long lost. Today we have Parts Two and Three to explore for the first time. They are a breath-taking assembly of materials, inspirational and life-changing writings expanding our appreciation of Isaac's wisdom and insight into the spiritual adventure.

The translations of Isaac's works that are available are expensive scholarly works, with detailed annotations. The purpose of this book is to make such precious translations accessible to the spiritual seeker—to allow Isaac here to speak for himself so that his words of wisdom may be received in the souls of those who read them and challenge and enrich contemporary practices of Christian spirituality. While scholarly articles and theses have been published, no work in English explores the implications for spirituality and the contemporary life of prayer from Isaac's Parts Two and Three. This book aims to meet that gap and to complement from the point of view of spirituality the popular and substantial theological study by Hilarion Alfeyev, *The*

Spiritual World of Isaac the Syrian, CS 124 (Kalamazoo, MI: Cistercian Publications, 2000), published before Isaac's Part Three became available in English. There are no resources published that relate Isaac's most recently discovered texts to contemporary spirituality.

This book has been written with the personal encouragement of Dr. Sebastian Brock, leading Syriac scholar and translator from the University of Oxford. He has spoken of the need to promote an appreciation of the Syriac tradition among an audience wider than specialists, so to help integrate awareness of the Syriac tradition as "the third lung" for the church. The Sankt Ignatios Theological Academy reminds us, "For the sake of Syriac's rich tradition and culture, Brock has called for a 'haute vulgarization' of the sources—historical, literary and theological—to broaden awareness and knowledge to a larger constituency."[2]

Spiritual Relevance

A brilliant writer, Isaac has the gift to put into words and describe the inner movements of the human spirit and Divine Spirit in prayer. He addresses themes that have strong resonances in our postmodern world:

- the quest for the Divine,

- spirituality as a never-ending adventure and voyage,

- the need for courage, imagination, vulnerability, and expectancy,

- the theme of hiddenness in prayer: mystery, and things hidden that can be revealed,

- writings that spring from his spiritual experience,

2. <sanktignatios.org>.

- cosmic breadth of vision,

- a capacity to stretch and expand us beyond usual limits and boundaries,

- a movement beyond conventional prayer practices into the Beyond,

- compassion for all humans and all creatures on the planet,

- ideas that are ecumenical and understandable by all traditions in the churches.

Dr. Brock has written of Isaac, "Although he wrote primarily with his fellow monks and solitaries in mind, almost all of what he has to say is applicable to all Christians in whatever walk of life."[3]

Ecological Relevance

Physicality and spirituality inter-relate, and one speaks to another. Working with these symbols of grace while thinking of the ocean will sensitize us to issues concerning the ecology of the ocean, so gravely under threat by contamination and pollutants today. As we reflect on the ecology of the soul and the treasures of the deep, we are alerted afresh to the urgency of preserving fragile undersea ecosystems, deepening our respect and reverence for the planet's seas. Many in the West were first intrigued by the oceans through the pioneering work of Jacques-Yves Cousteau, a French naval officer, oceanographer, and film-maker, who shared his findings in *The Silent World: A Story of Undersea Discovery and Adventure*, published in 1953, and in the unforgettable

3. Sebastian Brock, "The Syriac Tradition II: St Isaac of Nineveh," *The Way* 21, no. 1 (Jan. 1981): 68.

movie *The Silent World,* in 1956. More recently viewers have been captivated by the stunning photography of David Attenborough's BBC series *Blue Planet.* As we ponder the spiritual challenge of discovering the hidden depths of God's ocean of grace, we are reminded of today's ongoing exploration of the ocean and worldwide efforts at conservation. Isaac calls us to a sacramental way of seeing the world, appreciating the world as sacrament, the physical world revealing the Divine.

Now it is time to take the plunge and allow ourselves to sink into the mysterious ocean of the spiritual life. We are becoming spiritual swimmers, divers, and explorers of the depths of God! Isaac is calling us to be open-hearted and intrepid pilgrims and seekers as we set sail on an unforgettable voyage guided by his wisdom and experience, which newly speak to us across the centuries.

Outline of Contents

1. Becoming Explorers: an initial look at the Syriac tradition leads us to see what Jurgen Moltmann calls "mystic metaphors," which have the potential to open up to us astonishing discoveries in the spiritual journey.[4] We ready ourselves to accept Isaac's invitation and summons.

2. Quitting the Shoreline: we leave behind the securities of *terra firma* as Isaac shows us how the ocean becomes an image both of the Divine and of the human soul. We board the ship of the soul for a voyage of a lifetime!

3. Learning to Swim: we can go no further until we hear from Isaac his ideas about what makes a good swimmer and spiritual diver.

4. Jurgen Moltmann, *The Spirit of Life: A Universal Affirmation* (Minneapolis: Fortress Press, 2001), 285.

4. Risking the Depths: we start to appreciate Isaac's imagery of going out into the deep, and we encounter a central paradox in prayer: God is both hidden and revealed, treasure buried and unearthed, concealed and awaiting our discovery.

5. Facing the Currents: we start to understand the conflicting currents of the deep as we discover Isaac's teaching on the stirrings of the soul.

6. Embracing Transitions: Isaac maps out for us the different levels of prayer, as we prepare to sink deeper into a silence that beckons, toward the Beyond. The extended prayer exercise in this chapter invites us to take the plunge into the mysterious waters of prayer and make fresh discoveries for ourselves.

7. Diving Deep: we delight at the sort of pearls we might discover in such depths of prayer. As we marvel at gifts of revelation, insight, and wonderment, we learn what pearls Isaac himself unearthed.

8. Homecoming: our closing chapter celebrates our arrival in the harbor of rest as we share Isaac's hopes of the Life of the Age to Come—what he calls the New World—which we can experience even here, below, as we live on the edge of eternity.

Appendix 1 offers biblical resources to which Isaac alludes to use in times of prayer or retreat.

Appendix 2 offers practical guidelines on leading a retreat or quiet day with this material. It outlines possible timetables for retreats of a day, one night, or two nights, with suggested prayer exercises and resources for worship. In addition, it shows how this material can also be adapted for a retreat in daily life, whereby the participant works with material and prayer exercises set by the prayer guide and subsequently meets with the guide for a time of reflection and discernment. For these different kinds of retreat, participants will benefit from purchasing the book.

INTRODUCTION: FOUR SCENES

The Marketplace

Glinting and glistening in the Middle Eastern sun, it caught the eye of Jesus the teenager. He had never noticed these before. He loved the Jerusalem markets in his annual Passover trips to the holy city, and he would always find time to explore the bazaar. His senses were assaulted by the sights and smells, the colors and textures of the goods on sale. He admired the ceramics, the shiny metalwork, the wooden crafts, the fresh smell of citrus fruits and vegetables. But today his eye alighted on something he'd never seen before, small but shimmering, strangely sparkling, glowing and gleaming with an otherworldly sheen, lustrous, radiant with light. He asked the trader where it came from. "Divers," he replied, "find them in the Red Sea. How much will you give for one?"

Later, while in Galilee in his thirties, Jesus uttered a parable that has intrigued generations: "Again, the kingdom of heaven is like a merchant in search of fine pearls; on finding one pearl of great value, he went and sold all that he had and bought it" (Matt 13:45, 46). Jesus smiled as he recalled the merchant he had met in the marketplace in his teens. For him, the pearl seemed the perfect image to convey how precious is the Reign of God. The picture of a diver and a merchant intrigued and inspired him, as he thought of their determination, single-mindedness, full-hearted commitment, as he pondered the theme of the spiritual search, the

1

quest for truth, a sense of utter openness to fresh discoveries and adventure—what would they find? It seemed the perfect image to communicate to his hearers the need for alertness and for hearts that are seeking, an odyssey of the soul that stumbles on the greatest reality of all in the whole universe: the kingdom of God, the reign of heaven. Wow, says Jesus, we must be like an obsessive merchant who will never give up in his quest for the perfect pearl! We must stay ever open to fresh discoveries, new revelations of grace, even new epiphanies of the Divine, breaking out in unexpected places! Jesus loved the image of a buzzing marketplace where a person can either find great things or miss great things: "But to what will I compare this generation? It is like children sitting in the marketplaces and calling to one another, "We played the flute for you" (Matt 11:16, 17).

The Beach

As a child growing up in the seventh century Isaac loved the warm waters and the soft sand that fringed the coastal villages of Beth Qatraye on the islands of Qatar and Bahrain on the northeast coast of the Arabian Peninsula, an important center of Christianity at that time.[1] While flat rocky deserts stretch inland, the coast is edged with sandy dunes and, in places, beautiful mangrove forests. Like any child he delighted in splashing and playing in the inviting seas. But as he grew up, he realized that the sea was not only a playground; it was a place of industry. The crystal-clear waters that embrace Qatar enfold a diversity of treasures

---

1. See Mario Kozah, Abdulrahim Abu-Husayn, and Saif Shaheen Al-Murikhi, eds., *The Syriac Writers of Qatar in the Seventh Century* (Piscataway, NJ: Gorgias Press, 2014). Extracts are to be found in Brain E. Colless, *The Wisdom of the Pearlers: An Anthology of Syriac Christian Mysticism*, CS 216 (Kalamazoo, MI: Cistercian Publications, 2008).

to be discovered. Azure waters teem with a huge variety of species, such as barracuda, kobia, sheri, and snapper. Isaac would watch as the fishermen beached the boats and hauled in their great catches.

But he was especially intrigued by the divers. They went out into the open sea, and they had no nets among their cargo. At a distance, he could just see them plunging into the warm waters, where they seemed to disappear for ages without a breath, exploring the undersea world with their fingertips. Occasionally, but not often, as they returned to the surface they let out a great cheer and held aloft some precious find. These cries of excitement and exhilaration remained with the young Isaac all his life. As he grew up, he learned that what they had retrieved were precious iridescent pearls, hidden away like gems in a rockface, not easy to find but by their rarity and translucent beauty a delight and joy to the searcher.

With the enigmatic saying of Jesus resonating and reverberating in his soul, as Isaac's faith deepened and matured, he realized that the waters of the deep held many secrets and parables for the spiritual life. Later, when he sought the solitary life of a monk at Beth Huzaye (Elam), in the mountains of Khuzistan (today in southwestern Iran), after a brief time serving as bishop of Nineveh (present-day Mosul) in the 660s, his mind and heart returned to this childhood scene. The waters of the deep would yield to him rich treasures of imagery as he sought to put into words the wonders and discoveries of the spiritual adventure. Though finding himself amid desert and mountain, such memories repeatedly met in a creative interplay with imagination and accumulated wisdom, to produce some of the most inspirational spiritual treatises ever composed, treatises that retain their power for spiritual searchers today.

After a few years spent in solitude Isaac stayed in the community of the monastery of Rabban Shabur. Here he experienced a creeping loss of vision, resulting from his long hours studying texts of Scripture, so monks from Rabban Shabur wrote down prayers he had created and conversations they had had with him. They also stored his works for many years, guarding them as a treasure of their monastery. The value placed by Persian monasteries of the time on reading and writing is recorded from accounts in *The Book of the Governors (The Monastic History)* by Thomas of Marga (840), saying that many Persian monasteries at this time restricted admission to novices who were literate and could read. Jules Leroy explains the implications of this rule: "This arrangement meant that by the Middle Ages the Nestorian [Church of the East] monks had a passion for anything written. The libraries of the coenobia were always well stocked, not only with books of the scriptures or of the liturgy, generally in rich bindings, but also in ascetic and even profane literature . . . . the numbers varied from library to library, depending on the monastery, its importance, site, the generosity of the faithful, and the diligence of its copyists. No catalogue of a complete monastery library has been preserved."[2]

The Mountains

Yaroo M. Neesan was born in 1853 in the village of Katoona in Northwestern Persia (Iran). Because of vicious attacks by Kurdish peoples he was forced to flee as a child, with his family, to Urmia, where he lived on a farm. There was a significant Assyrian Christian population in this town, with churches and monasteries, and Urmia was also the site of the first American Christian mission in Iran in 1835.

---

2. Jules Leroy, *The Monks and Monasteries of the Near East* (London: Harrap & Co., 1963), 162.

As a young man Yaroo came under the influence of Presbyterian missions in the area and committed himself as a Christian. Working as a teacher at Tabriz and helping out on missions as an evangelist, he found his gifts and potential recognized, and the door opened for him in 1882 to study at the General Theological Seminary in New York. Ordained into the Episcopal Church in 1888, he was invited by the Archbishop of Canterbury to take a leading role in the Archbishop's Mission to the Assyrian Peoples. The archbishop began this venture in 1886, moved by the desperate plight of Syriac Christians belonging to the Church of the East in Persia, who were suffering appalling persecution and suffering.

During this ministry Yaroo became aware of the precious heritage of the Syriac Christians, represented in ancient manuscripts and parchments kept in monasteries and stored in forgotten cupboards in churches. He realized that these were in danger of being lost forever, because ferocious marauding tribes and bandits from the Kurdish peoples repeatedly ransacked the monasteries and burned down churches and libraries. It is not known from which monastery he rescued the document we now call Part Two of Isaac's corpus. What attracted him to this thousand-year-old document, which dates from the tenth century? What hardships did he suffer in order to bring this astonishing text to safety? Certainly considerable risk was involved. *The Christian Herald* contains testimony about one such rescue in the 1870s:

> He was invited to join a [Presbyterian mission party] . . . into the Koordish Mountains, where they were going with money, clothes and books to relieve the prevailing distress amongst the Koords consequent upon the famine and to preach the gospel and distribute Christian books. . . . The assistance of Mr Neesan was especially valuable . . . on account of his familiarity with the language of the Koords.

One night when the party was encamped in two tents on the outskirts of a village, a deacon of the mission church came out to them and spent the evening. As darkness fell, the alarm, sadly familiar to Mr Neesan's ears from his childhood, was given "The Koords are coming!" Instantly he was upon his feet to protect his charge. He had two old-fashioned pistols and an axe, and with these he advanced upon the brigands. The deacon and the cook came to his assistance and the Koords received a warm reception. The deacon soon fell, shot in the back, and the cook was wounded in the head, but the young student continued to fight against the robbers. The sound of the shooting was heard in the village and a number of the villagers came to the scene of the struggle. Not knowing in the darkness how many brigands might be engaged, they deemed it the wisest course to remove the ladies [missionaries] and the wounded deacon to the village for safety. They were accordingly hurried away. They could not find Mr Neesan and feared that he must be killed.

Returning upward of an hour afterward they were rejoiced to find him in the tent. He was a pitiable sight. For three hours he had maintained his fight in the dark and was badly bruised and wounded. One wound in the jaw was bleeding profusely, and his hands and face and clothing were covered in blood.

In their alarm they begged him to return with them to the village, but having succeeded in beating off the robbers, he was disinclined to leave the mission property as a prey, in the event of their return. He therefore picked up the most valuable part and sent it onto the village by the men and bade them return as quickly as possible for another load which he would have ready for them when they came back. On their return they found the Koords again advancing on the tents, and they proposed to stay still until the brigands came close, when they might kill them. Mr Neesan, however, interfered. That was not the missionary method, he said. . . . The party therefore fired their guns in the air, and the robbers realizing that their intended victims had been reinforced, were scared away. The work of transporting the contents of the tent was then continued, and Mr Neesan remained until the last bundle had been packed and was safely on the way to the village. Then he followed and his wounds were dressed . . . [they] completed their journey under the protection of a guard of Persian soldiers whom the Shah had sent to put down the brigands.[3]

This account gives testimony to Neesan's sacrificial efforts in safeguarding sacred books in the most testing and taxing of conditions. The article goes on to record how he retrieved and rescued a copy of the New Testament in Syriac, dated 1207 and written on parchment bound in ancient wooden covers. It also resonates strongly with a narrative written by Ernest Budge regarding his visit to Rabban Hormuzd monastery, a hundred miles or so southwest of Urmia in 1890, testifying to the vulnerability of such manuscripts:

The library of the monastery formerly contained a number of very valuable manuscripts but about the year 1844 the Kurds swooped down upon the monks and pillaged and set fire to the buildings and murdered all who opposed them. The monks succeeded in removing about 500 manuscripts to a house or vault on the side of a hill nearby, but unfortunately, a heavy flood from the rain from the mountains swept them and their hiding place away and nothing more was seen of them. A large number of manuscripts were also destroyed by the Kurds, who cut and tore them up before the eyes of the monks and who having destroyed

3. *Christian Herald* 9, no. 51 (Dec. 23, 1886): 802. See also J. F. Coakley: "Yaroo M. Neesan, a Missionary to His Own People," ARAM 5, nos. 1, 2 (1993): 87–101.

various portions of them hurled them down into the
stream which flows down from the mountain on one
side of the monastery. [Even today the monks] in the
mountains are threatened by destruction by marauding hill tribes which rob and plunder unchecked by
any.[4]

Neesan lived in Urmia in the nineteenth century, when
it became the center of a short-lived Assyrian renaissance,
with many books and newspapers being published in Syriac. Around 1900, Christians made up more than forty per-
cent of the city's population. However, in 1918 most of the
Christians fled because of World War I's Persian Campaign
and the Ottoman Empire's Armenian and Assyrian geno-
cides; thousands of ancient manuscripts, an inestimable part
of the Syriac heritage, were destined to be burnt and utterly
destroyed. During that period Neesan served on the archbishop's mission for almost twenty years, until 1918.[5] It was
to be a taxing task. Toward the end of the First World War,
in August 1918, he led 100,000 Assyrian Christians across
the Persian sands to British protection in Baghdad. The
refugees faced appalling massacres on the way; only half
of them survived the journey.[6]

A few years before, however, Neesan had taken from
Urmia a mysterious ancient manuscript with a provenance
from the region of northern Mesopotamia, secreting it in a
place of safety. Where did he take this precious document?
What was its destiny? What was its identity?

4. Ernest Alfred Wallis Budge, *The Histories of Rabban Hormizd the Persian and Rabban Bar-Idta* (London: Luzac, 1902), xxiii.

5. See J. F. Coakley, *The Church of the East and the Church of England: A
History of the Archbishop of Canterbury's Assyrian Mission* (Oxford: Clarendon Press, 1992).

6. *New York Times*, September 25, 1937: 17.

The Library

The scholarly silence of the library was for a long moment shattered. Normally broken only by the shuffling of papers and hushed, whispered requests and restrained, reverential conversations with the librarian, now it was disturbed by a deep gasp, a sharp intake of breath. The scholar rubbed his eyes in disbelief.

In 1898, while Neesan was on leave in England, he had deposited the precious Syrian manuscript in the Bodleian Library in Oxford, where it remained unread for almost a hundred years. The Bodleian, the main research library of the University of Oxford, founded in 1602, has over twelve million items. In April 1983 Professor Sebastian Brock, Reader in Syriac Studies at the University's Oriental Institute, requested from the archives of this vast treasury a document that intrigued him, identified only as MS. syr.e.7. As he looked at the manuscript, he could hardly believe his eyes, slowly beginning to realize that he held before him a work that scholars feared had been long lost:

> I was there collating a manuscript against a printed text for someone and had got rather bored. Seeing that I needed a break, I leafed through the card index of uncatalogued Oriental manuscripts in the Bodleian. My eye caught on one that had something like "Isaac of Nineveh, c.11th century." It was probably the early date that primarily suggested to me it would be fun to order it up. I wondered: it might have a colophon [an inscription at the end of a manuscript] saying where it was written. It did! An hour or so later it appeared, a small tightly bound volume on parchment in an East Syriac hand, of the approximate date on the card. It had lost its beginning, but I saw that in the colophon it said it was "the second half" of Isaac's writings. I could not at the time remember which half

was already known, so it was not till I got home and looked the details up that I found out that it was indeed the lost part—that had sat in the Bodleian for just about a century undetected!

Needless to say, it was one of those rare exciting moments of discovery that I have been fortunate enough to have had with manuscripts. Of course, if one makes such an exciting discovery, one is really obligated to do something about it, so as much as possible of vacations for the next ten years were spent preparing the edition and translation. Familiarizing myself with Isaac's writings and with the related East Syriac monastic literature was a wonderful opportunity for me to discover the riches of this tradition. Once the edition and translation were out, this put me in touch with quite a number of wonderful people, especially from different Orthodox Churches, who were interested in translating the new text into other languages. I find that Saint Isaac is one of the few monastic Fathers who is able to speak over the centuries in a relevant way.[7]

Now for the first time, English readers could discover for themselves the treasures that Isaac had penned in the seventh century.

Third Part

In another library, three thousand miles from England, in Iran, just a few years after Dr. Brock's discovery, an astonishing find was made, even further expanding knowledge of Isaac's writings. In a Jewish antiquarian bookshop in Teheran, the Chaldean archbishop of Teheran, Monsignor Yuhannan Samaan Issayi, a noted writer, linguist, hymnist,

---

7. I am grateful to Dr Brock for this account, which has not been published before.

and pastor, stumbled upon the Third Part of Isaac's writings. This new material was a 1903 copy of a manuscript probably from the fourteenth century, itself now long lost. Thus this copy was for decades considered unique, as the only known surviving version of Isaac's third volume.[8] After the archbishop's death in 1999, Fr. Michel van Esbroek, SJ, discovered this manuscript of the Third Part of Isaac's works in the archbishop's personal library in Teheran. Fr. Esbroek, an Oriental scholar and linguist from Belgium, had an insatiable hunger and keen eye for precious manuscripts.[9]

Fr. van Esbroek photographed the manuscript he had found in the archbishop's library and sent microfilm copies to various scholars in the field. Eventually Fr. Sabino Chialá, of the Community of Bose, Italy, edited and translated it; as he had earned a doctorate at Louvain la Neuve on the manuscript tradition of Isaac's known works, he was an ideal person to carry out this project. Later Mary Hansbury, who had close ties with a different Italian religious community, used his edition and Italian translation to render Isaac's Third Part into English for the first time, publishing it in 2016.

The present book now for the first time explores the implications for contemporary, lived spirituality from the seventh-century writings so recently rediscovered.

Isaac himself saw the composing of such precious documents as a metaphor for the spiritual life:

---

8. Grigory Kessel, "The Manuscript Heritage of Isaac of Nineveh: A Survey of Syriac Manuscripts," in *The Syriac Writers of Qatar in the Seventh Century,* ed. Mario Kozah, Abdulrahim Abu-Husayn, and Saif Shaheen Al-Murikhi (Piscataway, NJ: Gorgias Press, 2014).

9. For example, during 1976 he spent four months in the USSR visiting the libraries of Moscow, Leningrad, Tbilisi, and Yerevan, bringing back to the Bollandist Library in Brussels some 150 packages of books and some 7,000 manuscript photos.

Dealings in this world resemble a copy of a book which is still in rough draft. What a man desires or whenever he wishes, something can be added to or taken from it, and so he may alter his writing. Future dealings resemble documents drawn up as bonds, provided with the seal of the king, to or from which it is not allowed to add or subtract anything. As long as we are in the place where altering is possible, let us observe ourselves; and while we have authority over our life-book and our book is still between our hands, let us zealously add acts of beautiful behavior, and let us scratch from it the loss of the old behavior without freedom. We are allowed to scratch out faults, as long as we are here. And God will take into account every alteration we make in it. May we be deemed worthy of life everlasting before we appear before the king, and He puts His seal on the book. (1/LXII:292)

Sources and References

First Part

Ascetical Homilies of Saint Isaac the Syrian. Trans. Dana Miller. Boston, MA: Holy Transfiguration Monastery, 1984; revised 2nd ed., 2011. Cited as, for example, [Part] 1/ [chap.] 62: [page] 301.

Mystic Treatises by Isaac of Nineveh. Trans. Arent Jan Wensinck. Amsterdam: Nieuwe Reeks, 1923.

This translation is based on Paul Bedjan's Syriac text and is available online at archive.org and atour.com. Cited as, for example, [Part] 1/ [chap.] XX: [page] 109.

Second Part

Isaac of Nineveh: The Second Part, Chapters IV–XLI. Trans. Sebastian Brock. Corpus Scriptorum Christianorum Orientalium. Leuven: Peeters, 1995.

Cited as, for example, [Part] 2/ [chap.] X: [paragraph] 32.

Third Part

Isaac the Syrian's Spiritual Works. Trans. Mary Hansbury. Piscataway, NJ: Gorgias Press, 2016.

Cited as, for example, [Part] 3/ [chap.] XX: [paragraph] 4.

Note: Isaac was writing in the first instance for male monks, so he frequently uses the male pronoun, though his teachings are in fact fully gender-inclusive and for all.

Questions for Reflection

1. What are the origins and sources of your spiritual practice?

2. What is the most precious part of the tradition—that is, what has been "handed on" to you—that you would cherish and preserve at all costs, so it could never be lost or forgotten?

3. What is your experience of Eastern Christians so far?

4. What do you know about the Syrian Orthodox Church and the Church of the East?

5. What do you know of persecuted Christians in the world today?

6. How do oppressed believers preserve their inheritance of faith?

7. What do you know of the present churches in Iran and Iraq?

1. Becoming Explorers

My beloved ones, because I was foolish, I could not bear to guard the secret in silence, but have become mad, for the sake of your profit. . . . Oft when I was writing these things, my fingers paused on the paper. They could not bear the delight which had fallen into the heart. (Isaac the Syrian, 1/LXII:288)

What Are You Looking For?

Above all else, Isaac invites us to become explorers of the Divine. His key theme and desire is *movement*—he longs for us to keep going forward in our spiritual search and encounter an ever deeper knowledge of the Divine. He summons us to a transformative life-changing journey that leaves behind inherited theoretical, rational knowledge of divine things and leads us into firsthand experiential knowledge—knowing God, not just knowing about God. The former way of knowledge is discursive, enjoying discussion; the latter is intuitive and leads to silence and wonderment. The first is focused on gaining information, but the second is about being in formation, reshaped by God's grace. The first is marked by external debate, the latter characterized by receptivity to God's gifts of revelation and inspiration.[1] Isaac's

---

1. See Valentin-Cosmin Vesa, "The Doctrine of Knowledge in Isaac of Niniveh and the East Syriac Theology of the 7–8th Century," dissertation, University of Padova, 2015.

life states his priorities. He did not want to throw himself headlong into the christological controversies of his time and the Nestorian debates in the Church of the East. He wanted to seek God in prayer.

Isaac wants us to rejoice in our God-given capacity for the Divine. He wants us to realize that the human person has a faculty for receiving revelations and fresh vision. There is a fluidity in his terminology: through our heart, through our intellect / mind, and through the practice of contemplation or *theoria*, we are able to welcome life-transforming insights into God and ourselves. In Isaac the words of Evagrius of Pontus (346–399) come true: "The one who prays is a theologian; a theologian is one who prays."[2] Prayer becomes perception: we start to see things differently, and life will never be the same again.

At the same time that Isaac was writing, in the Byzantine tradition Maximos the Confessor was affirming, "When the intellect (*nous*) practices contemplation, it advances in spiritual knowledge . . . the intellect is granted the grace of theology when, carried on wings of love . . . it is taken up into God and with the help of the Holy Spirit discerns—as far as this is possible for the human intellect—the qualities of God."[3] As Maximos explains, such knowledge is transforming: "The intellect joined to God for long periods through prayer and love becomes wise, good, powerful, compassionate, merciful and long-suffering; in short, it includes with itself almost all the divine qualities."[4] Later

---

2. *Evagrius Ponticus: The Praktikos and Chapters on Prayer*, trans. John Eudes Bamberger, CS 4 (Kalamazoo, MI: Cistercian Publications, 1972), 65.

3. Maximos the Confessor, "Four Hundred Texts on Love," in *The Philokalia*, translated by George E. H. Palmer, Phillip Sherrard, and Kallistos Ware (London: Faber & Faber, 1981), 2:69.

4. *Philokalia* 2:74.

traditions will speak of "relocating the mind to the heart."[5] In his own way, Isaac will show us how this is possible.

A Sense of Adventure

Isaac's teaching on the three phases of spiritual journeying is the subject of chapter six. For the moment, let's celebrate his view of our capacity and potential to make progress as we enter different intensities, and three deepening forms of knowledge. He begins with the basics, and a working knowledge of human weaknesses and passions: this is discursive philosophical knowledge. But we can advance to the stage of soul and enjoy the deepening of our knowledge of God through contemplation, which becomes a form of perception: here knowledge is more intuitive and experiential. His third step approaches the fullness of divine knowledge, a foretaste of heaven, whetting our appetite for the Life of the Age to Come:

> Excellent is that one who remains alone with God: this draws him to continual wonder at what is in His nature. . . . Also concern increases for the new world and care for future things, earnest meditation on these things and continual migration, which is the journey of the mind to these things. (3/I:8)

---

5. Later Simeon the New Theologian writes of moving or relocating the mind to the heart: "The mind should be in the heart . . . . Keep your mind there (in the heart), trying by every possible means to find the place where the heart is, in order that, having found it, your mind should constantly abide there. Wrestling thus, your mind will find the place of the heart" ("Three Methods of Attention and Prayer," in E. Kadloubovsky and George E. H. Palmer, *Writings From the Philokalia* [London: Faber & Faber, 1977], 158).

Isaac's idea of "continual migration" conveys a sense of journeying and movement in the spiritual life. In the same opening chapter of Part 3 he raises the great themes of searching and discovery:

> There is nothing which is capable of removing the mind from the world as converse with hope; nothing which unites with God as beseeching His wisdom; nothing which grants the sublimity of love as the discovery of His love for us. There is nothing which lifts the mind in wonder, beyond all which is visible, to abide with Him far off from the worlds, as searching the mysteries of His nature. (3/I:16)

There had been caution in the Syriac tradition about the idea of a spiritual search, but Isaac is its fearless advocate. Isaac wants us to wake up and become alert to new possibilities of grace. He sees that the process of knowing God is an evolution and a progression, as we develop our spiritual faculties and become ever more open to the Divine.[6] But how can he communicate these life-changing truths and discoveries?

Communicating the Mysteries of the Soul

How can we describe to others what is happening to us on our spiritual journey? How can we depict, for the benefit of ourselves and for others, the spiritual road that we are taking: experiences of prayer, transitions that we travel through, impediments that we face? William Barry and

6. See also Serafim Sepälä, "The Idea of Knowledge in East Syrian Mysticism," *Studia Orientalia* 101 (2007): 265–77; Sebastian Brock, *Spirituality in the Syriac Tradition* (Kottayam: St. Ephrem Ecumenical Research Institute / SEERI, 1989); Patrik Hagman, *The Ascetism of Isaac of Nineveh* (Oxford: Oxford University Press, 2011).

William J. Connolly write, "most people are inarticulate when they try . . . to describe their deeper feelings and attitudes. They can be even less articulate when they try to describe their relationship with God. . . . For to begin to talk about this aspect of their lives requires the equivalent of a new language, the ability to articulate inner experience."[7]

In his study of religious metaphor Joseph Campbell writes, "Here we sense the function of metaphor that allows us to make a journey we could not otherwise make."[8] As we seek to bring to expression aspects of our inner, spiritual life, we discover that we need metaphors, frameworks, reference points. Jurgen Moltmann affirms how vital it is to use images to describe spiritual experience: "In the mystical metaphors, the distance between a transcendent subject and its immanent work is ended . . . the divine and human are joined in an organic cohesion."[9]

The Syriac tradition brims with a bold, imaginative, and creative approach to religious language and imagery as it seeks to communicate and put into words the knowledge of the Divine being discovered in prayer. Syriac writers develop an astonishing theological sensitivity to their environment, and discover a spiritual language from the natural world, where physicality points to spirituality.[10] The spiritual writers are at once theologians and poets.

---

7. William A. Barry and William J. Connolly, *The Practice of Spiritual Direction* (New York: Seabury Press, 1982), 67.

8. Joseph Campbell, *Thou art That: Transforming Religious Metaphor* (Novato, CA: New World Library, 2013), 9.

9. Jürgen Moltmann, *The Spirit of Life: A Universal Affirmation* (Minneapolis: Fortress Press, 2001), 285.

10. Robert Murray, *Symbols of Church and Kingdom: A Study in Early Syriac Tradition* (London: T & T Clark International, 2006). He celebrates images in the Syriac tradition borrowed from environment and the natural world, such as vineyard, grape, tree of life, rock.

In terms of theological sources, Isaac of Nineveh is most indebted to John of Apamea (known as John the Solitary, from the fifth century), Evagrius (346–399), Theodore of Mopsuesta (350–428), and Diodore of Tarsus (d. 390). He also appreciated the writings attributed to Dionysius and Macarius. But in terms of his imagery and metaphors, Isaac was inspired not only by John of Apamea but also by the great poet and hymn writer Saint Ephrem the Syrian (ca. 305–373), a pioneer of daring language and metaphor. Isaac inherited Saint Ephrem's astonishing sacramental worldview, in which the whole created order brims with the Divine and teaches us about God's ways. This is not a utilitarian approach to the natural world, looking around for helpful illustrations of or analogies for the spiritual life. Rather, it is a question of training oneself to recognize the revelatory character of creation and how God teaches us through it:

> Lord, Your symbols are everywhere . . .
> Blessed is the Hidden One shining out. (*On Faith* 4.9)[11]

The Syriac tradition encourages people to read the two books of nature and Scripture. Ephrem affirms:

> The keys of doctrine
> which unlock all of Scripture's books,
> have opened up before my eyes
> the book of creation,
> the treasure house of the Ark,
> the crown of the Law.
> This is a book which, above its companions,
> has in its narrative
> made the Creator perceptible

---

11. Sebastian P. Brock, *The Luminous Eye: The Spiritual World Vision of Saint Ephrem the Syrian*, CS 124 (Kalamazoo, MI: Cistercian Publications, 1992), 55.

and transmitted His actions;
it has envisioned all His craftsmanship,
made manifest His works of art. (*Hymns on Paradise* VI.1)[12]

In his book Moses
described the creation of the material world,
so that both Nature and Scripture
might bear witness to the creator:
Nature, through man's use of it,
Scripture, through his reading of it.
These are the witnesses
which reach everywhere,
they are to be found at all times,
present at every hour. (*Hymns on Paradise* V.2)[13]

Ephrem's writings burst out with an awesome variety of symbol and metaphor: the way, wedding feast, physician, medicine of life, mirror, pearl, tree of life, paradise. For Ephrem and others the goal of the sanctified life is the recovery of the paradisiacal state, when Adam and Eve were still clothed in the "Robe of Praise." The Robe of glory is a key metaphor. In the incarnation, God clothes Himself in a body. In ongoing divine revelation, God clothes Himself in words:

He clothed Himself in language, so that He might clothe us in His mode of life. (*On Faith* 31.2)[14]

It is language, then, that reveals, empowers.

Isaac stands in such a tradition with its sensitivity to the environment and responsiveness to Scripture. He delights

---

12. St. Ephrem the Syrian, *Hymns on Paradise,* trans. Sebastian Brock (Crestwood, NY: St Vladimir's Seminary Press, 1990), 108–9.

13. St. Ephrem the Syrian, *Hymns on Paradise,* 102–3.

14. Brock, *Luminous Eye,* 43–44.

in "the ocean of symbols of God's economy [saving plan]"
(2/XI:24).

Metaphors Enable Us to Be Spiritual Explorers

Metaphors have the power to shift us from left-brain ana-
lytical thinking to creative right-hemisphere imagining—
and imaging. Paul Avis points out that metaphors drawn
from the natural world are used by poets as a hermeneutical
key to help map the landscapes of the mind: "Metaphor is
generated in the drive to understand experience . . . .
Metaphor is not just naming one thing in terms of another,
but seeing, experiencing and intellectualizing one thing in
the light of the other."[15] Brian Wren puts it this way: "Metaphors can . . . extend language, generate new insights, and
move us at a deep level by their appeal to the senses and
imagination."[16]

In his study *The Edge of Words: God and the Habits of Language*, Rowan Williams summons readers to be unhesitating
in their use of metaphors: "So as we take more risks and
propose more innovations in our linguistic practice, we
move from the more-or-less illustrative use of a vivid and
unusual simile through to increasingly explosive usages
that ultimately . . . invite us to rethink our metaphysical
principles, our sense of how intelligible identities are con-
structed in and for our speaking. Extreme or apparently
excessive speech is not an aberration in our speaking."[17]

15. Paul Avis, *God and the Creative Imagination: Metaphor, Symbol and
Myth in Religion and Theology* (London: Routledge, 1999), 97.

16. Brian Wren, *What Language Shall I Borrow? God-Talk in Worship* (London: SCM, 1989), 92.

17. Rowan Williams, *The Edge of Words: God and the Habits of Language*
(London: Bloomsbury, 2014), 130.

Metaphors stoke and trigger the imagination. Janet Martin Soskice affirms their cognitive role, aiding and deepening our understanding of things: "what is said by the metaphor can be expressed adequately in no other way . . . the combination of parts in a metaphor can produce new and unique agents of meaning."[18] Metaphors evoke and stimulate rather than define or confine. Metaphors help to unify and integrate experience, because they link the spiritual to the physical and the soul to the body, enabling the metaphysical to become physical.

So too Isaac the Syrian urges his hearers to rediscover the sacramentality of words: like bread and wine they can bear God's presence and reveal the Divine—so words should be approached with reverence and appreciation. Soskice affirms that "The sacred literature . . . both records the experiences of the past and provides the descriptive language by which any new experience may be interpreted."[19]

Isaac Summons Us

In his writings, Isaac reveals his longing that we might experience more of God. Although his writings are called "mystic treatises" or "spiritual discourses" or "ascetical homilies," they are not dry abstract theorizing. Rather, he writes with a passion that springs from his own discovery of the Divine. He writes as a fellow pilgrim, companion on the journey. He offers advice as a spiritual friend—humbly

18. Janet M. Soskice, *Metaphor and Religious Language* (Oxford: Clarendon Press, 1985), 31. See also George Lakoff and Mark Johnson, *Metaphors We Live By* (Chicago: University of Chicago Press, 1980).

19. Soskice, *Metaphor*, 160. See also Andrew D. Mayes, *Learning the Language of the Soul: A Spiritual Lexicon* (Collegeville, MN: Liturgical Press, 2016).

offering guidance and encouragement. He urges us not to be timid or have low expectations of prayer.

With metaphors Isaac wants to unlock our imagination and help us start to see things differently. He talks about prayer in terms of birthgiving (2/IV:7), opening doors (2/V:8), spiritual inebriation, intoxication with God (2/V:4). Vitally, Isaac knows that there is a potential in metaphor properly described as *heuristic:* "stimulating further investigation, encouraging discovery through experimenting, exploration of something by first-hand experience." Through his nautical, maritime, and underwater imagery Isaac invites us to a certain playfulness, an uninhibited creativity. He says, in effect, "come on—let's see where this leads us." As we see in the next chapter, it leads us to the depths.

Prayer Exercise

Take some time to express and articulate your longings, spiritual and vocational, in terms of one or two metaphors that rise to the surface of your consciousness. Echo Isaac's newly discovered prayer:

> O Sun of righteousness by which the righteous have beheld their own selves and become a mirror for their generations, open up within me the gate to awareness of You; grant me a joyful mind, one which sails above the rocks of error . . . . Stir up within me the vision of Your Mysteries so that I may become aware of what was placed in me at holy baptism. . . . Rig together my impulses for the ship of repentance, so that in it I may exult as I travel over the world's sea until I reach the haven of Your hope. (2/V:13, 14)

Questions for Reflection

1. As this voyage of discovery begins, what are you seeking?

2. What kinds of knowledge are important to you right now?

3. What metaphors emerge when you begin to describe the course of your spiritual life over the last year?

4. What kind of metaphors do you tend to use most easily? Why is that, do you think?

5. What do you think can stimulate the art of wondering—reflection, musing—about God's presence in your life?

2. Quitting the Shoreline

Now that we have found an unexplored ocean and an un-
limited treasure, should we desire to stay at a poor foun-
tain? O unspeakable richness, o ocean rich in its billows
and in its amazing treasures. (1/LI:244, 245)

Isaac beckons us onward and outward, leaving our safe
havens and venturing toward the deep. He longs for us to
become intrepid voyagers, vigilant navigators in the spiritual journey. Horizons and depths now summon us to an
adventure of discovery. It is a quest: we will move "from
island to island and from knowledge to knowledge." There
is no turning back:

> The sailor gazes at the stars as long as he is sailing on
> the ocean, and he directs his ship by them, that they
> may show him the harbor. The monk gazes at prayer,
> which directs his way showing him towards which
> harbor he has to direct his course. At prayer the monk
> gazes at all times, that it may show him the island
> where he may anchor his ship free from fear and where
> he may take on board provisions in order to direct
> himself towards another island. Such is the course of
> the solitary as long as he is in this life. He departs from
> island to island, and from knowledge to knowledge.
> And at various islands he meets the various kinds of
> knowledge, till he goes ashore and directs his course
> towards the city of truth, the inhabitants of which do
> no longer traffic, but every one is content with his

goods. Blessed is he whose course is not disturbed on
this wide ocean. Blessed is he whose ship is not
wrecked and who reaches that harbor with joy.
(1/XLV:218)

As Isaac recalls the azure blue waters lapping the islands
of the Gulf, and the beckoning far horizons shimmering in
the heat of the sun, he sees the ocean as an image and metaphor of three things. First, it suggests to him an image of
God, a picture of God. Second, it comes to represent the
ambivalence and paradoxes of the ocean of this world. Third,
it speaks to him of the state and potentiality of his own soul.

The Ocean of God's Grace

For Isaac God's love is immeasurable, unfathomable,
boundless, without limit and beyond all understanding.
The ocean comes to represent the immensity of God's inexhaustible love, his mystery and power. It speaks of divine
fecundity and abundance. Isaac's thought is always over-
whelmed by the experience of God's love. It is the source
and basis of his theological discussions, ascetical explanations, and mystical insights. Isaac longs that we might experience the grace of God inundating and saturating our
parched soul. He testifies, "The flood of Christ's mysteries
presses upon my mind like the waves of the sea . . . . Your
mystery stupefies me" (2/V:19).

Isaac beckons us to launch ourselves into such an ocean.
Four invitations emerge:

Explore the Mystery

What unspeakable riches, a swelling ocean rich in
wondrous treasures, the overflowing power of faith!
How full of consolation it is, and how pleasant and
reassuring its course is. (1/XL:245)

Isaac wants us to embrace an ocean of divine knowledge and experience for ourselves "the waves of his goodness":

> Why have we abandoned this Fountainhead of life and Ocean of knowledge, wandering off on earth engaged in our own affairs and the things that involve us, with the result that we are thrown night and day into struggles, contests and fights with the thoughts, the passions, memories and their provocations, while we have the means to cause all these things to dry up without a struggle simply by turning? (2/X:26)

> The wealth of His love and power and wisdom will become known all the more—and so will the insistent might of the waves of His goodness. (2/XXXIX:6)

> I turn back to look at [His mysteries] as they have become a great ocean before me, limitless to cross and pleasant to behold. (3/V:12)

Enjoy the Compassion

For Isaac wonderment at God's creativity blends with awe at God's mercy. The ocean represents for him the immensity of God's creative power: "With the assistance that comes from grace, let us . . . approach the riches of God's nature and the ocean of His creative power and the waves and resplendence of His Being" (2/IX:13). But creativity is inseparable from compassion:

> Let us consider, then, how rich in its wealth is the ocean of His creative act, and how many created things belong to God, and how in His compassion He carries everything . . . how compassionate God is, and how patient; and how He loves creation . . . . Then, once someone has stood amazed, and filled his intellect with the majesty of God, amazed at all these things He has

done and is doing, then he wonders in astonishment at His mercifulness. (2/X:19)

He asks, "Who can measure the vast depth of God's compassion?" (2/XXXIV:1).

How wonderful is the compassion of God!—who can measure the ocean of His grace? (2/XIX:11)

But the ocean of the grace of God, who confesses it as his due? (3/VI:1)

O Ocean of compassion, rescue me from the anxiety of wandering away from You. (3/VII:20)

What mercy not able to be measured!
What sea of total compassion!
What grace without limit!
What love, greater than the world! (3/X:96)

Experience Forgiveness

The seas also embody for Isaac the promise of God's cleansing power:

O Ocean of pardon, begin to wash nature's uncleanness from me and make me fit for Your sanctuary. (3/VII:34)

As a handful of sand thrown into the ocean, so are the sins of all flesh compared with God's mind. (1/L:231)

We judge even the great ocean of Your love which with its waves exceeds the measure of all our iniquity. (3/VII:40)

Paradoxically, it can seem at times that human sinfulness extends further than oceans of grace, but this is not so:

The waves of the sea are less
than the number of my sins,
but if we weigh them against Your love,
they vanish as nothing. (3/X:101)

Encounter the Grace

The exuberance of God cannot be measured. Contemplating
the natural world gives Isaac an expansiveness of vision, a
worldview characterized by God's all-embracing love, a
cosmic perspective:

> The one who truly recognizes that God's goodness is
> the cause of his joy . . . . His joy comes to be more
> abundant than the sea, because it is the goodness of the
> God of the universe affording such joy, and all creation
> is a partaker in it, even sinners share in this. (3/VI:16)

> Seeing that His face is set all the time towards forgive-
> ness. . . . He pours over us His immense grace that,
> like the ocean, knows no measure. (2/XL:13)

Rejecting any idea that God looks for retribution and re-
taliation for man's sinfulness, Isaac declares God to be "the
fountain of love and the ocean full of bounty" (1/XLV:216).

Isaac addresses God as the ocean: "O Ocean that has sustained the world, draw me out of the stormy sea" (3/VII:21).
He sees an image of God's gift of peace in still waters, de-
claring that "the smoothness of the ocean of the peace of
His Nature is not perturbed by any contrariness on our
part" (2/X:23).

The Ocean of the World

From time to time storm surges terrify the waters of the Gulf
where Isaac grew up. The sea level can rise and fall by

several meters because of ferocious winds associated with the Shamal system, coupled with changes in atmospheric pressure, topography, and tidal effects. Isaac had seen these with his own eyes, and now, in later life, he discerns in them a picture of a storm-tossed world:

> Many ships have gone astray in this ocean [the temporal world] . . . . despite the wearisome and laborious toils of their steersmen, and the astonishing nature of their knowledge, they have been unable, in their goal, to spurn this world—which involves a mortified heart, consisting in humility and no thought about oneself. (2/XX:21)

> Whenever the helmsman intellect [ruling mind] encounters the temptations of the world, it resembles a steersman who was sailing calmly on the sea, with a gentle following wind blowing him towards harbor, when all of a sudden he finds himself on a reef. (2/XVII:12 = 1/LV:265)

As there are hidden dangers in the sea, so the mariner-soul must be alert to the spiritual risks associated with pride:

> Glory on the part of worldly folk is like a rock hidden in the sea; it is not known to the sailor before his ship is split on it so that its bottom is pierced and it is filled with water. (1/XLV:219)

> Isaac finds himself praying, "Grant me a joyful mind, one which sails above the rocks of error." (2/V:13)

So too the ambivalence of sea speaks of the challenge of the spiritual voyage. Its changing moods and conditions cloak the wonders of the deep:

> Those who have done the crossing of this ocean are aware of the winds that blow there. (1/XXXVIII:121)

Many are the variations of this sea. Who knows its toils
and the multitude of merchandise, the wondrous
pearls in its deeps, and the creatures that rise up from
within it? Blessed is he who does not slumber during
his voyage. (1/XXXVII:219)

So the sea becomes a place of paradox—an image of
God's grace but also a picture of struggle:

What then? Varying states happen to every man, like
[changes of] the air. Understand it: to every man; for
nature is one. Do not think that he [Macarius of Alex-
andria] is speaking to insignificant men only and that
the perfect should be exempt from varying states and
that they stay in one class, without liability of deviation
and without the impulse of the affections . . . . He
says: there are states of cold, and soon after states of
heat; and perhaps of hail, and soon thereafter of serenity. It is thus for our instruction: strife, then the help of
grace. And sometimes the soul runs into a storm and
heavy billows assail it; then there comes a different
state and it is visited by grace; then joy fills the heart
and peace from God and chaste, peaceful delibera-
tions. (1/LXXII:333)

If thou doest fall into temptations, do not despair. For
there is no merchant who travels on seas and roads
without suffering losses; and there is no husbandman
who simply reaps the whole; and there is no champion
who suffers not blows and strokes even if he gains
victory in the end. So in the things of God, in the things
of the merchants who go this invisible road, there are
profits and losses, blows and victory. When thou art
hit, do not turn thy back. (1/LXXX:378)

Isaac is a realist, and he knows firsthand the passions that
Christians face, their trials and temptations: "Our soul is
then suffocated and, as it were, in the midst of storms"

(1/XLVIII:227). We face doubt and are buffeted by anxious thoughts and fears. We find ourselves praying,

> Encourage, our Lord, our souls
> with the hidden voice which comes from the stillness,
> when You teach us, by means of the Spirit,
> the hidden aim of our struggle.
> May our mind not be lacking
> in Your encouragement, our Savior,
> lest it be drowned in the sea
> by the waves which cut off hope. (3/X:79, 80)

Such waves threaten to destabilize and discourage us, but the stillness of God teaches and reassures us:

> To You we call out from the waves,
> O our wise Mariner:
> cause to blow on us a serene breeze,
> but if we sink, draw us out. (3/X:60)

In the image of the ocean as this passing world, Isaac draws attention to a sense of vulnerability and exposure experienced by the spiritual seeker. The turbulence and swell, bearing flotsam and jetsam—and, we would add today, pollutants—become an evocative picture of life in the world. The seeker needs to develop vigilant skills in navigation. So Isaac needs to pray, "Send Your power, my Lord, to assist me and rescue me from the sea of temporal life. O Sea of help, continue to help me and do not abandon me to the abyss of evils" (3/VII:19). Changing the image, he hails God as "My Creator and my Hope, the Anchor of my life in the midst of storms" (2/V:21). And he holds on to the hope: "Blessed is he whose voyage is not disrupted on this wide ocean. Blessed is he whose ship is not wrecked and who reaches that haven rejoicing" (1/XXXIII:218).

The Ocean of the Soul

If the ocean faces dragons, it also embraces dolphins:

> Just as the dolphin stirs and swims about when the
> visible sea is still and calm, so also, when the sea of the
> heart is tranquil and still from wrath and anger, mys-
> teries and divine revelations are stirred in her at all
> times to delight her.
>
> When our Lord desires to give us initiation to the spiri-
> tual mysteries, he opens wide in our minds the ocean
> of faith.[1]

As Isaac reflects on the liquidity of the soul, he develops
his thinking around the dual themes of limpidity and luminosity.

Limpidity

Again and again Isaac returns to an unusual phrase: *limpidity* or *limpid purity of heart* (*lebba shaphya*). It denotes God's
call to us to discover the clear, unpolluted, and uncluttered
waters of the soul. It evokes a sense of stillness and trans-
parency in the waters of the soul that might be contrasted
with a condition where our inner life seems more like cha-
otic, murky, muddied waters churned up by anxiety or by
unnecessary attachments—what Isaac calls "the dark mist"
(1/LXIV:305). God wants to lead us from agitated, cloudy
waters to crystal-clear waters, where the silt and the debris
settle to the bottom, as it were, and the waters of the soul
become unclouded, receptive, and open to divine revelation.
The phrase alludes perhaps to the text, "your voice has
surely been heard by the Most High; for the Mighty One

---

1. 1/15:85, trans. Miller.

has seen your uprightness and has also observed the purity that you have maintained from your youth" (2 Esdras 6:32). Isaac reflects:

> Any soul into whose nature there is no entry for in-
> creased anxiety about amassing goods does not require
> great care to find by and in itself impulses of wisdom
> about God. . . . For when outside waters do not enter
> into the fountain of the soul, its natural waters spring
> up—wondrous thoughts are they, which are continu-
> ally moved toward God . . . its natural limpidity and
> innocence. (1/3:1, 2, 12)

Clear waters of the soul—its "natural limpidity"—can be regained as, reflecting on divine compassion, one rediscovers a sense of one's own identity in God:

> Let the scale of mercy always be preponderant within
> you, until you perceive in yourself that mercy which
> God has for the world. Let this our state become a
> mirror where we may see in ourselves that likeness
> and true image which naturally belong to the Divine
> Essence. By these things and their like we are enlight-
> ened so as to be moved toward God with a limpid
> understanding [clear mind, Wensinck]. (1/64:312,
> trans. Miller)

Isaac adds, "A merciful man is the physician of his own soul; for he drives away from his inner being the dark mist, as by a strong wind" (1/LXIV:305).

In the Third Part Isaac writes of both limpidity of mind and limpidity of soul:

> by [means of] the labors of the heart in stillness . . .
> the mind arrives at the limpidity of the labor of the
> mind. (3/I:6)

> the mind is lifted from the passions and the battles,
> likewise from labor, by means of that sublime recol-
> lection in God. . . . This takes place in freedom from
> all the things of this life and in limpidity of the intel-
> ligence, which is more exalted than the world. All these
> realities are within the light of the mind. (3/XV:11)

> When the soul has become limpid, immediately on
> encountering some subject about God, in that moment
> the mind is compelled to silence, a spiritual fervor
> arises in it and a quiet, amazed love. (3/IV:24)

Isaac is explaining that when we let go of the cares and
struggles of this world, its passions and conflicts, our mind
and thoughts can reach a clarity, a new sense of freedom.
We reach a calm and restful place where we experience
greater receptivity to hidden truths and see things more
clearly. We once again enter clear waters, not waters choked
or clogged by flotsam and jetsam and detritus.

Luminosity

Reflecting on the ocean of the soul, Isaac reassures his hearers that dark waters can be penetrated by rays of sunlight,
as it were, and become translucent waters—light bearing:

> Luminous meditation on God is the goal of prayer . . .
> the fountainhead of prayers, in that prayer itself ends
> up in reflection on God. (2/X:38)

> Excelling reflection, combined with glorious converse
> with God is something which only a few are found to
> have acquired, having done so through the luminosity
> of their thoughts, and thanks to the grace of Christ.
> (2/X:31)

Worship aids this process of becoming translucent waters: "by being meditated upon, [psalms and hymns and chants] give birth within us to pure prayers and exalted insights, thus bringing us close to luminosity of mind and wonder at God, as well as to all the other things with which the Lord will enlighten you with wisdom in their due time" (2/XXI:7).

We take a further look at Isaac's teaching on illumination in chapter five. Here, let's celebrate the light-bearing potential of the sea of the soul and Isaac's conviction that "little by little some spaciousness of heart is born" (2/XXXIV:2).

The Ship of the Soul

Isaac, then, urges us to get ready to sail and to climb on board:

> The mind that has found spiritual wisdom is like a man that has found on the ocean an equipped ship which, when he has got aboard, brings him from the ocean of this world to the island of the world to be. Just so the apperception of the future things in this world, is like a small island in the ocean. And he that has approached unto it, he will be no more vexed by the storms of temporal phantasies. (1/XLV:217)

> So it is becoming for us, as the blessed Mar Ephraim says, that we make our soul resemble at all times a ship prepared [for sea]. When the wind [required] for her will blow, she does not know . . . . how much more is it becoming for us to be prepared and ready. (1/LXII:292)

Isaac delights in the image of the ship of repentance. He prays, "Rig together my impulses for the ship of repentance, so that in it I may exult as I travel over the world's sea until I reach the haven of Your hope" (2/V.14).[2]

---

2. He also writes of "The weary ship of . . . ascetic conduct" (2/VII:3).

In developing this image Isaac talks about such a boat having a rudder of fear to guide it:

> As it is not possible to cross the ocean without a boat or a ship, so no one can cross towards love, without fear. This foetid sea, which lies between us and the intelligible paradise, we cross in the boat of repentance, which has fear for a rudder. If the rudder of fear does not govern this ship of repentance, in which we cross the sea of this world towards God, we shall be drowned in the foetid sea. Repentance is the ship, fear is her governor, love is the divine port. Fear places us in the ship of repentance and makes us cross the foetid sea of the world and brings us into the divine port which is love, towards which look all those who are weary and crushed by repentance. (1/XLIII:212)

By fear, Isaac does not mean a state of anxiety before God but rather deepest reverence, as in Proverbs 1:7. In his First Discourse he writes, "The foundation of man's true life is the fear of God" (1/I:2). This is the rudder that guides us toward the ocean of the love of God. It is a starting point, which leads us toward a realization of the wonder of God. We move from fear to love.[3]

---

3. In his review of Patrik Hagman's *The Asceticism of Isaac of Nineveh* (New York: Oxford University Press, 2010), Sebastian Brock observes, "Hagman indeed identifies fear as being for Isaac 'the most important motivator towards living the life of the ascetic' (p. 114) . . . . an entire chapter is devoted to 'Fear as the existential background of asceticism'. It would seem that, for Isaac, in order to overcome the fear of death—the sense of malaise engendered by the life of 'the world'—it is necessary to acquire 'the fear of God'. Since this phrase in Syriac often just renders Greek εὐσέβεια, the meaning could denote little more than a religious awareness, but Isaac certainly means much more than this, and Hagman is right to see behind this term a movement from what Isaac calls 'knowledge on the level of the body' to 'knowledge on the level of the soul'" (*Journal of Theological Studies* 65, no. 1 [April 20]: 320–23).

The important thing is to keep moving in the spiritual journey. Isaac recalls the experience of the Desert Fathers:

> Abba Arsenius, for the sake of God . . . chose silence and solitude. Thus he voyaged with the spirit of God on the ocean of this world in the ship of solitude, in exalted peace . . . . It appears to me ridiculous to talk about mastering the course of solitude without abandoning all things and the care of all things. (1/XVIII:104)

In a rare poem,[4] Isaac prays for safe passage toward the harbor of rest:

> In early morning, when sailors
> begin to work in the world,
> in Your harbor, my Lord, our souls
> are at rest from all stirrings. (3/X:10)

> Our body is for us like the sea
> which always submerges our boat:
> bring near, our Lord, our ship
> to Your divine harbor. (3/X:30)

Questions for Reflection

1. How do these images resonate with your own experience?

2. What images or pictures of God are you drawn toward? How do you find yourself responding to Isaac's image of the Ocean of God?

4. Isaac's authorship of this poem is sometimes doubted by scholars.

3. What image of soul or self do you find yourself working with most often—your default self-understanding? What do you learn from Isaac's ideas of the ocean of your soul?

4. What is your experience of being saturated, inundated, drenched by grace or forgiveness?

5. What is your experience of stormy waters leading you closer to God?

6. If your soul were a ship or vessel what kind would it be? (Confident oceangoing liner, refugees' vulnerable dinghy, tanker, fishing boat?) What is this image telling you?

7. How seaworthy and equipped is your "ship of repentance"? How would you describe it (sparkling, refurbished, battered, stable)? What preparations are needed before you can set sail?

Prayer Exercise

1. What is your experience of the sea of your life? What dangers or challenges have you faced in your spiritual voyaging? Where have you been—with God? How has the sea of your soul ebbed and flowed? Chart and chronicle your progress.

On a fresh piece of paper draw a personal timeline to recall the voyages you have made thus far. Draw a wavy horizontal line to represent, as it were, the surface and intersection between public events in your life and the hidden private, personal world below the surface. Mark between the peaks of the waves the decades of your life.

Above the line, note major events and transitions, including new jobs, house moves, births and deaths, new ministries.

Below the line try to note how you felt, beneath the surface of events, in the depths of your soul. How did you experience God at these moments or phases of your life?

Celebrate your spiritual voyaging thus far "from island to island and from knowledge to knowledge." How far have you come?

Bring this to a close by giving thanks for God's providence in your life, and entrust your future to him. Conclude by reading aloud Isaiah 43:1-2: "Do not fear, for I have redeemed you; I have called you by name, you are mine. When you pass through the waters, I will be with you."

Or

2. Imagine—picture in your mind's eye, as vividly as you can—a vast ocean spreading in front of you as you stand on the shoreline, reaching out to a distant horizon. Let this sea represent your life before God. Describe the sea for yourself.

Is it expansive, rough, hectic, tempestuous? Are there rolling, pounding, heaving, crashing, choppy waves? Foamy, frothing, and spraying crests? A squalling gale or stillness like a millpond? Is your sea calm, with expectant doldrums, or quiet undulating waves, or stillness? What color is the sea—deep blue, turquoise, gray?

Recall the images that Isaac offers us: "an ocean of grace," "a swelling ocean rich in wondrous treasures," "sea of total compassion!" "the ocean of this world."

Then ponder: What is the ocean of your soul like, now?

You may like to draw a picture or sketch to express both your ocean and your type of ship (see question 6 above).

3. LEARNING TO SWIM

. . . dive into sea of stillness. (2/XXXIV:5)

What makes a good spiritual swimmer?

> But when bodily thoughts have to some extent been
> lifted up, then impulses manifest themselves wholly
> in the spiritual sphere, swimming in the heart of
> heaven with incomprehensible things. (1/III:19).

> Great is this mystery! I do not know how I had con-
> ceived to swim in this great ocean and who had given
> me these strong arms for swimming with pleasure in
> the unfathomable abyss without being wearied. But
> seeing that the ocean is wide and its limit not visible,
> the more the arms are imbued with pleasure and in-
> stead of fatigue, joy leaps up from within the heart.
> (3/V:16)

It is time for us to learn the art of spiritual swimming.
Isaac is urging us to take the plunge and hold back no longer. He speaks of God's call:

> dive into the sea of stillness
> alight on the richness of the sea
> descend to the heart of the earth
> descend to the depths which bear riches. (2/XXXIV:5, 12)

What skills and attitudes are required of the spiritual swimmer? What does Isaac teach us about spiritual fitness, about getting into condition? In this chapter we identify the six vital skills and attitudes that Isaac says we need: determination, training, spiritual disciplines, flexibility, holding the breath of our thoughts, nakedness, and vulnerability. Then we will be ready to sink, swim, and explore the depths.

Determination

Isaac wants us to realize that spiritual swimming takes determination, effort, and struggle. It is no easy path, no soft option. Indeed, as we noted when thinking of the changing moods of sea and ocean, spiritual swimming entails embracing risk and danger—it takes a sort of spiritual courage. Isaac gives warnings against sloth or about hopes of quick and easy discoveries. We need steadfastness and persistence:

> If the diver found a pearl in every oyster, then everyone would quickly become rich! And if he brought up one the moment he dived,
>> without the waves beating against him,
>> without any sharks encountering him,
>> without having to hold his breath until he almost expires,
>> without being deprived of the clear air which is granted to everyone else,
>> and having to descend into the abyss—
> if all this were the case, pearls would come more thick and fast than lightening flashes! (2/XXXIV:4)[1]

> In the case of divers, they will very often go down and find oysters consisting of just ordinary flesh; only once

---

1. In Isaac's time, it was thought that a pearl is created in an oyster by strikes of lightning penetrating the oyster's open edges.

in a while will there be a pearl in it. Their experience
is also ours in the commerce which consists in prayer:
barely a single one occurs through us wherein there is
consolation for our weariness. (2/XXXIV:6)

Singlemindedness sustains our hope of great discoveries
in prayer and prepares us to face spiritual dangers and risks:

> And as the eyes of the helmsman look to the stars, so,
> in all his long and difficult labors, the inner gaze of the
> solitary, during his whole course, is directed towards
> the aim which he has fixed in his mind the first day
> when he gave himself to sailing the rough sea of soli-
> tude, til he shall find the pearl for the sake of which he
> has entrusted himself to the not-to-be explored floods
> of the ocean. And his gaze of hope makes light to him
> the whole burden of service and the difficulties full of
> danger which meet him in his course. (1/LXVI:314)

There is no merit in holding back from the labors of
prayer, trying to avoid practices of prayer that can be de-
manding, exhausting as well as reinvigorating:

> And if, because our pearls seem to our eyes easily
> come by and small by comparison with those of the
> Fathers, or if we hold back from the fatigues of the sea,
> and cease entirely from our eagerness, then we will
> never learn about the swimming which is involved in
> prayer . . . nor will we descend to the depths which
> bear riches. (2/XXXIV:12)

The spiritual adventure entails cost and even a measure
of suffering:

> If you do not possess lowliness of heart, or the sweet
> and burning suffering that comes with the love of God,
> things that are the root for those tears which pour forth

delectable consolation in the heart, then do not take
refuge in the excuse of any lameness on nature's part,
or people whose heart is naturally torpid, and whose
interior members—which should put into motion in
the soul the healthy power of rationality—are impaired.
Do not use these as an excuse for not even feeling a
little suffering over your own deficiencies. (2/XVIII:14)

Playing with the analogy of physical fitness or lameness,
Isaac is urging us to face the personal cost, as it were, of
limbering up "the limbs of the soul."

Training

With experience we can know our potentialities and our
limits—we can, as it were, become self-aware of our ability
to swim spiritually:

Those who are skilled in the craft, who possess the experience of age and long practice in this labor, also
know how to make their body's movements dive down
to deep places where they can find superb and incom-
parable pearls of great price. Similarly, this happens
corresponding to the ability of the mind which swims
about in such places during the time of prayer—places
where it is not easy for everyone to swim. (2/XXXIV:7)

We can take heart—God equips us and strengthens our
weary limbs. Isaac speaks of the divine energy inhabiting
us. It is "in His glory and in His energy that He abides [in
the soul] . . . . It is the power and energy of God that sancti-
fies and sets apart from the other souls that soul in which
the Lord is sanctified" (3/VIII:13).

The word *ascetical*, used to describe the first Christians
who went into desert spaces to seek God face to face, comes
from the Greek *ascesis*—meaning training or discipline. Isaac

talks of training in "the stadium of uprightness" (2/X:1), evoking the image of the Olympian athlete in Paul:

> We all know that when there's a race, all the runners bolt for the finish line, but only one will take the prize. When you run, run for the prize! Athletes in training are very strict with themselves, exercising self-control over desires, and for what? For a wreath that soon withers or is crushed or simply forgotten. That is not our race. We run for the crown that we will wear for eternity. So I don't run aimlessly. I don't let my eyes drift off the finish line. When I box, I don't throw punches in the air. I discipline my body and make it my slave so that after all this, after I have brought the gospel to others, I will still be qualified to win the prize. (1 Cor 9:24-27, trans. *The Voice*)

How strong a swimmer are you, spiritually? Do you feel spiritually fit? Or maybe carrying excess weight? As Hebrews puts it:

> Therefore, since we are surrounded by so great a cloud of witnesses, let us also lay aside every weight and the sin that clings so closely, and let us run with perseverance the race that is set before us, looking to Jesus the pioneer and perfecter of our faith, who for the sake of the joy that was set before him endured the cross, disregarding its shame, and has taken his seat at the right hand of the throne of God.

It goes on to talk of the need for *ascesis*:

> Our human parents disciplined us for a short time as seemed best to them, but God the Father of spirits disciplines us for our good, in order that we may share his holiness. Now, discipline always seems painful rather than pleasant at the time, but later it yields the

> peaceful fruit of righteousness to those who have been
> trained by it. Therefore lift your drooping hands and
> strengthen your weak knees, and make straight paths
> for your feet, so that what is lame may not be put out
> of joint, but rather be healed. (Heb 12:1-2, 10-13)

Swimmers use every major muscle in their bodies—
swimming is a full-body exercise—that is why it is so good
for us, and recommended for all ages and as a therapy. As
we grow in confidence as spiritual swimmers, we develop
the ability and capacity to flex our spiritual muscles and
make bold strokes rather than tentative nervous ones. We
come before God in prayer humble, but not timid: "Let us
therefore approach the throne of grace with boldness" (Heb
4:16). But we need practice and the discipline of regular
periods of silence and expectant receptive prayer. We need
to build into our lives a spiritual fitness regime, perhaps
with the help of a trainer, a mentor, or a spiritual director
or companion. Traditionally prayer practices have been
called spiritual exercises—those that might stretch us spiritually. In his first letter to Timothy, Paul is emphatic:

> Train yourself in godliness, for, while physical training
> is of some value, godliness is valuable in every way,
> holding promise for both the present life and the life
> to come. (1 Tim 4:7, 8)

The *Message* translation puts it:

> Exercise daily in God—no spiritual flabbiness, please!
> Workouts in the gymnasium are useful, but a disci-
> plined life in God is far more so, making you fit both
> today and forever. You can count on this. Take it to
> heart. This is why we've thrown ourselves into this
> venture so totally.

Isaac tells us that God is our primary trainer, in these words of reassurance:

> God trains them as a man who teaches swimming to a little boy; as soon as he begins to sink, the teacher lifts him up, for the boy swims upon the hands of his teacher. And when the courage of the boy begins to diminish, from fear that he will be drowned, the man who supports him with his hands cries: "be not afraid, I support thee." . . . So God's grace will bear up and train the children of man, namely those who trust themselves clearly and simply to the hands of him that created them and who with their whole heart turn from the world and follow him. (1/XXXVI:183)

Fear paralyzes, but faith liberates. As we learn to swim spiritually, we enjoy a certain liberty. As we let go of weights and sin that clings so closely we enter into a spiritual freedom, enjoying unhindered movement. Maybe we can even dare to experiment in our forms of praying!

Spiritual Disciplines

Isaac commends a range of spiritual disciplines that keep us spiritually fit.

> We need to take the body seriously. It has the potential to be a temple where God's presence abides. (2/V:1)

Isaac develops this theme in Part 3, chapter VIII:

> Let us earnestly desire this good [knowledge of the mysteries] and continually sanctify the parts of our body, together with our soul, in the praise of God . . . . We become holy temples by prayer, to receive within ourselves the adorable action of the Spirit . . . .

> Sanctify your soul and all your limbs with His bless-
> ings, saying "Bless the Lord, O my soul; and all my
> bones, his holy name." (Ps 103:1, 3/VIII:14, 16)

The body needs to be kept in check. Once again, physicality points to spirituality: outward parts suggest the necessity
to attending to inward limbs. Isaac prays for release and a
sense of freedom, both inner and outer:

> O Unbinder of our nature, unbind from me the hidden
> bonds which have been cast around my interior limbs,
> and undo from my outer senses the manifest restraints,
> so that I may run to enter the Paradise of Your Myster-
> ies. (2/V:20)

Outward practices and labors with a physical dimension
include fasting and an attitude of detachment from material
things. We need to safeguard our outward senses by vigi-
lance and watchfulness so we can activate the inner senses:

> Make me worthy to taste of You, so that my eyes may
> grow light . . . . Cause Your hidden power to dwell
> in us, so that the senses of our souls may be strength-
> ened, in order that our soul may mystically strike up
> a song filled with wonder . . . may we bear on our
> hidden limbs the sanctification of Your divinity.
> (2/X:41)

> Make me worthy to behold You with opened eyes
> which are more interior than the eyes of the body. Cre-
> ate new eyes in me, You who created new eyes for the
> blind man. Close my exterior ears and open hidden
> ears, which hear the silence and the sounds of the
> Spirit. (3/VII:33, 34)

The body can be harnessed for prayer by way of prostrations—a key feature in Syriac worship[2]—and kneeling. The lips can be employed for the recital of the psalms. Recital of the Hours—the monastic Office—at regular points through the day—is recommended.

The reading of Scripture may prove transformational. Isaac writes of "the wondrous reflection sown in the intellect by the reading of Scripture and the search for hidden things . . . . The reading of Scripture manifestly is the fountainhead that gives birth to prayer—and by these two things we are transported in the direction of the love of God whose sweetness is poured out continually in our hearts" (2/XXIX:2, 5; see also 2/XXXIII:1–3).

In addition to reading Scripture, Isaac recommends other spiritual reading and the study of the Fathers as a source of spiritual wisdom and encouragement. Essential in Isaac's practice is reception of the "Divine Mysteries"—the Eucharist. The Sacrament, pearl-like, becomes a hidden treasure waiting to be discovered:

> Everyday we have embraced You in Your mysteries,
> and with our bodies we have received You. . . .
> You have hidden Your treasure with our body,
> by means of the grace which dwells
> at the elevated table of Your mysteries:
> grant us to see our being made new.
> Because, my Lord, we have buried You in ourselves,

2. In current Syriac practice, unchanged through the centuries, a prostration, made after each part of the prayer, is a full bow to the ground with the knees touching the ground and the head touching or near the ground, then immediately standing back up. As the bow to the ground is begun, the sign of the cross is made. Some people touch their knees to the ground first and then bend their upper body down, while others fall forward to the ground, knees and hands touching at the same time. "O God, cleanse me a sinner" is said twelve times, with a bow each time.

> having eaten at Your spiritual table,
> may we feel, our Lord, in that deed,
> the future renewal! (3/X:18, 20, 21)

The discipline of solitude is vital, and Isaac knows that it is easily eroded and needs to be safeguarded and ring-protected. The monk must know when to open the door of his prayer cell to others and when to keep it firmly closed from interruption (1/XLI:205f). Isaac talks here about maintaining boundaries and not transgressing "voluntary borders": "Doest thou further desire that thy beloved ones long after thee? See their faces at fixed days only" (1/XLI:209). For those of us who are not monks, the challenge is to balance availability to others and undistracted attentiveness to God. The two commandments, to love God and to love others, find themselves in a creative tension.

The aim of such disciplines is an increase in humility and openness to God: "the guarding of the heart is the most important thing of all" (2/XXIX:7). Spiritual disciplines are a place to return to in times of darkness or confusion, a kind of reference point and default position.

"Let us not be perturbed when we are in darkness . . . our soul is then suffocated and, as it were, in the midst of storms" (1/XLVIII:227). Sometimes we will face faintheartedness, lack of patience, humility, self-pity, anger, or other passions. At other times God permits us to face depression or doubt, and we are quite unsure of their origin. So we should train ourselves to go back to basics: to stay calm, wait, read Scripture, the Fathers, and hold on to liturgical prayer, as a kind of unchanging rock in the sometimes turbulent ocean of our soul.

Flexibility: Variety of Prayer Practices

Swimmers employ a range of different movements: the front crawl, breaststroke, butterfly stroke, backstroke, sidestroke. We need to loosen up and limber up for variety as spiritual swimmers. There is no need to get stuck or fixated in a particular way of praying.

Isaac recommends flexibility so that we might stay ever more responsive to God. Liturgy and the canonical hours of prayer, while vital, have the potential to become the springboard for meditation: "There are times when a person is transported from prayer to a wondrous meditation on God" (2/X:39). Isaac does not support slavish adherence to recital of the psalms. Liturgy and psalmody become a diving board for meditation as a person stays with a word or phrase that resonates in the soul. The psalms act as a catalyst and stimulus, sparking off thoughts, triggering meditation:

> If you are desirous of tasting the love of God, my brother, ponder, and with understanding meditate, on the things that pertain to Him and which have to do with Him and His holy nature: meditate and ponder mentally, cause your intellect to wander on this all your time, and by this you will become aware of how all the parts of your soul become enflamed with love, as a burning flame alights on your heart, and desire for God excels in you . . . . luminous meditation on God is the goal of prayer; or rather, it is the fountainhead of prayers, in that prayer itself ends in reflection on God. (2/X:29, 38–40)

If we stay open, psalmody might lead to meditation, and meditation becomes increasingly contemplative, as we move beyond active thinking to resting in God and maybe sailing into a harbor of rest. As we will see (chapters five and six), stirrings and strivings pass to silence and stillness.

Isaac especially commends devotion to the cross. It has become a locus of divine presence, once found in the tabernacle or temple of old:

> We look on the Cross as the place belonging to the Shekhina [glory] of the Most High, the Lord's sanctuary, the

ocean of symbols of God's economy . . . . Whenever
we gaze on the Cross in a composed way, with our
emotions steadied, the recollection of our Lord's entire
economy [plan of salvation] gathers together and
stands before our interior eyes. (2/XI:24, 26)

Isaac recommends keeping before us a visual presentation of the cross, which we can touch and connect with:

Whenever we gaze upon this image in the time of
prayer, or when we show reverence to it, because that
Man was crucified upon it, we receive through it divine power, and we are held worthy of assistance,
salvation and ineffable good in this world and in the
world to come—that is to say, in the Cross. (2/XI:13)

Holding the Breath of Our Thoughts

In the case of our feeble selves, whose swimming takes
place close to dry land, it is only these following small
pearls which come up for us . . . . These do so when
we dive eagerly, many times over, holding the breath
of thoughts of this world during our prayers and Offices. (2/XXXI:8)

Isaac is emphatic—we need to hold our breath—and cease
from speaking and talkative prayer. In another place he
writes, "A cloud covers the sun: so much talk covers the soul
that has begun to be illuminated by contemplative prayer"
(1/XLV:218). We need both to discover and then safeguard
silence. We need to quiet the overactive mind, so given to
discursive reasoning and buzzing with questions.

Spiritual Nakedness and Vulnerability

Naked the swimmer dives into the sea in order to find
a pearl.

Naked the wise monk will go through creation in order
to find the pearl, Jesus Christ Himself. (1/XLV:218)

What does Isaac mean when he writes of naked swimmers?

First he alludes to the radical degree of dispossession and detachment we need from earthly anxieties that would hold us back. We need to shed these. This idea evokes the very nudity of Jesus at the crucifixion—emphasized with detail in John's gospel (John 19:22-25). It is an image of the total self-giving of Jesus on the cross. The theme also recalls the image of Peter at Galilee in the days after the resurrection. His fishing while naked represents an unbridled search, a dedicated quest, not only for the treasures of the deep but for meaning and purpose in those disorientating days after the first Easter (John 21:7). While Syriac poet Ephrem emphasizes the human being clothed in baptismal garments of light,[3] here Isaac is inviting us to shed anything that would prevent us from approaching the Divine.

Sometimes Isaac speaks of "nakedness of the mind"— meaning a radical letting go and detachment from things the senses attract us to.[4]

> Bodily discipline in solitude purifies the body from the material elements in it. Mental discipline makes the soul humble and purifies it from the material impulses that tend towards decaying things, by changing their affectible nature into motions of contemplation. And this will bring the soul near to the nakedness of the mind that is called immaterial contemplation; this

3. *Saint Ephrem the Syrian: Hymns on Paradise,* trans. Sebastian Brock (New York: St Vladimir's Seminary Press, 1990).

4. See the Evagrian concept of "naked mind": "The naked mind (nous) is that which, by the contemplation which concerns it, is united to the gnosis of the Holy Trinity" (*Kephalaia Gnostica* III.6).

is spiritual discipline. It elevates the intellect above earthly things and brings it near to primordial spiritual contemplation; it directs the intellect towards God by the sight of unspeakable glory and it delights spiritually in the hope of future things, [thinking of] what and how each of them will be. (1/XL:202)

When the mind is in a state of natural steadfastness, it is in angelic contemplation, which is the first and natural contemplation which is also named naked mind. (1/III:21)

The last garment of the mind are the senses. Its state of nakedness is its being moved by kinds of non-material contemplation. Leave the small things in order to find the honoured ones. (1/III:22)

Second, Isaac refers to the vulnerability and openness of soul that are essential for an encounter with the Divine. Isaac beckons us, as it were, toward total exposure to the Divine, with no cover-up. Adam and Eve's nakedness can represent their primordial openness to God, while their making of loincloths symbolized not only a sense of guilt and shame but also represented both a fear and a barrier to God—a hiding, concealment from God: "But the LORD God called to the man, 'Where are you?' He answered, 'I heard the sound of you in the garden, and I was afraid, because I was naked; and I hid myself'" (Gen 3:9, 10). This image invites us to remove any materials behind which we might hide from God's penetrating gaze. Nothing must get between us and the waters of grace, the sea of total compassion. We swim in the nude!

In the fourth century Jerome said of the desert experience, "The desert strips you bare." He was referring to that degree of honesty and authenticity that true prayer demands. We must strip ourselves of our self-protective barriers. The false, competitive self must die. The self or ego identified with our outward *persona* (Greek: mask) that we present to the world must be shed, enabling us to come before God without defenses or pretenses.

Nakedness may have other connotations. Water flowing against bare flesh and naked skin, where there is no resistance or drag, means that there is nothing to slow a swimmer down. The nakedness then alludes to a freedom of spirit, a liberty of soul, a readiness for discovery, a full-bodied alertness to the Divine. Again, physicality gives clues to spirituality. We recall the enigmatic note in Mark 14 about the arrest of Jesus in Gethsemane: "A certain young man was following him, wearing nothing but a linen cloth. They caught hold of him, but he left the linen cloth and ran off naked" (Mark 14:51, 52). The Divine requires total relinquishment. As Isaac puts it, "And he who goes naked for His sake will be clad by Him with a garment of glory" (1/V:53).

Isaac encourages us to take the plunge and immerse ourselves in the ocean of grace. We need to cease clinging, as it were, to the side of the boat or to any securities that tie us down. It is time for us to leave our comfort zones and to let go—to allow ourselves to sink into the sea of compassion. We are poised now before the opportunity of utter self-abandonment and surrender to God.

It takes decisiveness and God-given resolution to release our grip. It is good to ask, "What holds me back?" We need to name our fears, or sense of unworthiness . . . .

As we look down into the deep waters below our "ship of repentance," we know there is a risk of struggle. Faith is taking the plunge. Scripture reassures us:

> The eternal God is your dwelling place,
> and underneath are the everlasting arms. (Deut 33:27, RSV)

> When you pass through the waters I will be with you.
> (Isa 43:2)

We sense that as well as illumination there is deep darkness in the depths. In the next chapter we'll explore echoes
in Isaac of ideas of darkness and shadows of unknowing—
the *via negativa*. While this may seem at first intimidating,
we may sense that the deepest spiritual discoveries may be
in the depths of darkness.

So, what is holding you back from plunging into the sea
of God's love, if anything?

Questions for Reflection

1. How would you express your resolve and goal as a spiritual swimmer?
2. What spiritual disciplines are shaping and forming you,
   helping you to be spiritually fit?
3. How flexible and daring are you in respect to trying out
   different ways of praying?
4. How can you "hold your breath" and find more silence
   in your life?
5. What does the image of spiritual nakedness say to you?
   Is there anything that you need to let go of?
6. What expectations do you have of your prayer times?
   What do you hope might go on in them?

Prayer Exercise

This chapter has drawn us back to essentials, to basics. We see what is important and necessary to sustain and energize the spiritual life, and what is not. From time to time Isaac stresses the need for recollection and remembrance of God's whole providential economy—or saving plan—his creation of humanity and his incarnation in Christ, and our hope of glory. Take time to name and celebrate the essentials of your faith. Name for yourself the elements and key truths that inspire you. And give thanks.

4. Risking the Depths

Dive down to deep places . . . descend to the depths
which bear riches. (2/XXXIV:7, 12)

With his experience of the inviting waters of the Gulf, Isaac testifies of an immersion in the depths of quiet:

> solitude sends me continually waves of gladness . . .
> which, running against the ship of my soul and with-
> drawing it from the sounds of the world and from the
> life of the flesh, immerse it in the deepest depths of
> quiet in God. (1/LXVI:314)

Isaac longs for us to seek "a deep intelligence, penetrating and attaining to the hidden things in all depths" (1/ XXXVII:188). He affirms, "the depth of the heart is stirred towards the praise of God" (2/XV:6). In wonderment "a mighty gasp ascends from the depths of the heart . . . that person is lowered to the abysses in his thoughts" (2/XXXII:1). Isaac delights to make his own the sentiments of the psalmist: "Let us . . . cry out in wonder How magnificent are the workings of Your providence, Lord; Your thoughts are profound indeed . . . . Your judgements are like the great abyss . . . . His ways cannot be fathomed" (2/XXXXIX:1; cf. Ps 92:5; 36:6; Rom 11:33). He asks, "Who can measure the vast depth of his compassion?" (2/XXXIV:1).

A Spirituality of Descent

Onward and upward? Paul writes about "the upward call of God in Christ Jesus" (Phil 3:14), and in the history of Christian spirituality the metaphor of ascent prevails: the image of going up to God.

Since the Tower of Babel in Genesis 11, people have located divinity in the sky: " 'Come, let us build ourselves a city, and a tower with its top in the heavens, and let us make a name for ourselves.' . . . The LORD came down to see the city and the tower, which mortals had built" (Gen 11:4, 5). Biblical stories of theophany—divine revelation—take place on mountaintops. The ark comes to rest on Mount Ararat. Moses receives the Torah amid mysterious cloud and darkness atop Sinai, and Elijah encounters God in the cleft of the rock on Horeb and welcomes the divine fire on Mount Carmel. The divine presence is located in the temple on Mount Zion. In the gospels Jesus is transfigured atop a high mountain (Tabor or Hermon) and makes his ascent to heaven from the crest of the Mount of Olives. Scholars have noticed that Matthew's gospel gives special prominence and meaning to mountains (and features them more than the other gospels do): the mounts of temptation, teaching, healing and feeding, transfiguration, end-time teaching, the mountain of the great commission.[1] Each mountain looks back to Sinai's revelation and forward to Zion, symbol of the end-time gathering.

The way to God seems to be up, up, up. Writing at his monastery at the foot of Mount Sinai, the holy mountain towering above him, the abbot John Climacus (579–649) suggests that the virtues form thirty rungs on the *Ladder of Divine Ascent*. The Franciscan Saint Bonaventure writes of

---

1. See, for example, Terence Donaldson, *Jesus on the Mountain* (Sheffield: JSOT Press, 1985).

the "mind's ascent to God" in his work *The Journey of the Mind into God*. In the English tradition Walter Hilton calls his account of prayer *The Ladder of Perfection*. Later Spanish mystic John of the Cross in his masterpiece *The Ascent of Mount Carmel* uses this model of going up to God and leaving worldly things behind. Sometimes, Isaac himself uses language of ascent, for example, writing of the ladder of prayer (3/IX:12, 13, 17) in reference to Peter's rooftop vision, and "the highest place of prayer" (3/IX:31) in reference to Moses on Mount Sinai.

The concept of ascent originates in Hebrew and Christian cosmology. It is the heavens that are "telling the glory of God" according to the psalmist.[2]

However, we can recognize the severe limitations of this model of prayer and discipleship.

Gregory of Nyssa (330–395) had delighted in the image of climbing mountains but wanted to make it very clear that an ascent to a summit of prayer is but a beginning, not an end. In his *Life of Moses* he traces a map of the Christian pilgrimage as it is suggested to him by the Exodus accounts.[3] It begins with baptism, prefigured in the crossing of the Red Sea, liberating a person from the captivity not of Pharaoh but of sin. The Christian pilgrim's journey, like the trek through the wilderness, will be marked by God's provision (as in manna, water from the rock), God's guidance (the pillar of cloud), human failure, and spiritual battles (as represented in the conflict with Amalekites). Ultimately all this leads to the ascent of the mountain of divine knowledge, represented in Sinai. But is this the final goal?

2. Ronald A. Simkins, *Creator and Creation: Nature in the Worldview of Ancient Israel* (Peabody, MA: Hendrickson Publishers, 1994).

3. See *Gregory of Nyssa: The Life of Moses*, trans. Abraham J. Malherbe and Everett Ferguson (New York: Paulist Press, 1978), 2:226, 227.

Gregory develops a dynamic view of spiritual development, characterized by *epekstasis*—a vision of the Christian life as continually evolving and progressing, energized by the Holy Spirit. His key text is the resolve of Paul: "Forgetting what lies behind, and straining forward [*epekteinomenos*] to what lies ahead, I press on toward the goal, for the prize of the heavenly call of God in Christ Jesus" (Phil 3:13-14). For Gregory, the disciple should never stand still, but continually stretch toward the "upward call" and so reach his or her full potential in Christ:

> the finest aspect of our mutability is the possibility of growth in good . . . let us change in such a way that we may constantly evolve towards what is better, being transformed from glory into glory, and thus always improving and ever becoming more perfect by daily growth.[4]

For Gregory, each stage reached in the spiritual journey is but a springboard into fresh adventures in prayer. The pilgrim can never say that he or she has arrived. In Gregory's eyes, the greatest sin is that of complacency, of resting on one's laurels. Gregory's vision is one of lifelong learning or, rather, eternal progress. In the *Life of Moses*, each new summit the patriarch conquers is but an invitation to see wider horizons and higher ascents to be made. But while the experience of prayer is an ongoing and never-ending journey in Gregory, we still seem to be climbing from peak to peak!

Today we recognize several shortcomings or dangers in the image of the spiritual ascent. Ascent resonates with the modern desire for ambition, self-advancement, self-

---

4. "On Perfection," in *From Glory to Glory: Texts from Gregory of Nyssa's Mystical Writings*, trans. Colm Luibheid and Norman Russell (London: John Murray, 1962), 51–52.

development, and the seeking of promotion, "going up the ladder," acquiring ever greater power and status. It invites comparison, competition. Ascent encourages us to think in terms of hierarchy. The goal is achieving success, spiritual attainment. It also seems to emphasize the place of human effort in the spiritual quest and downplay the role of the Divine. The model of descent, rather, leads us toward surrendering, sinking into God, letting go, unlearning . . . . This contrasts with ideas of ascendency and advancement—mastery, conquest of mountains, and, yes, prideful achievement. The idea of elevation of soul sounds like superiority. We notice a contrast between gritted determination and exertion required in climbing the mountain of prayer and a gentle sinking into the ocean of grace, as Isaac commends. Will we desire to sink or strive? Cling on or let go?

The predominating ascent model in spirituality also suggests that one must renounce the world and get away from it in order to find God. It depicts striving for a faraway heaven. It nurtures a divisive dualist worldview where heaven and earth are set in opposition. The further we climb away from the world, it seems, the closer we get to heaven.

A further, related contrast emerges in the issue of being in control. The image of the spiritual climber conveys the impression that the one making the ascent is in control, in charge of the venture, attempting as it were to conquer the mountain by pickax, one's safety and security reinforced by rope and harness, and attachments to a cliff-face where needed. The aim is spiritual conquest and accomplishment: competitive ideas of winning and reaching the summit sooner than others may not be far away. The contrasting image of the spiritual swimmer plunging into the depths seems to require a certain relinquishment of control, a releasing of our grip on securities—at once a playful, inquiring—and yes, a risky model of prayer. As we shall see, Isaac tells us to sink, not strive.

Isaac Celebrates the Descending God

Our God is a descending God. Paul celebrates the *kenosis* of the Word, which leads to his welcome in the underworld (Phil 2). He makes the astonishing descent not only from heaven to earth, but beyond: to under the earth. The writer of the letter to the Ephesians has a big question:

> each of us was given grace according to the measure of Christ's gift. Therefore, it is said, "When he ascended on high he made captivity itself a captive; he gave gifts to his people." When it says, "He ascended," what does it mean but that he had also descended into the lower parts of the earth? (Eph 4:7-9)

N. Gordon Cosby writes of the descending God, "If God is going down and we are going up, it is obvious that we are going in different directions . . . . We will be evading God and missing the whole purpose of our existence."[5]
Isaac marvels at the descent of God:

> Who will not wonder on seeing all these things which took place in Christ our Lord . . . who . . . of His own will and without any supplication or request from elsewhere came down to their abode and lived among them in their body just as one of them . . . . He has stooped down to such an extent that He is willing to be called "Father" of sinful human nature, dust from the earth. (2/XL:14)

For Isaac contemplating this divine descent inspires deepest humility and casts aside all thoughts of prideful achievement:

---

5. N. Gordon Cosby, *By Grace Transformed: Christianity for a New Millennium* (New York: Crossroad, 1998), 31.

Humility is the garment of the Divinity, for the Word
which became man put it on and spoke in it with us,
through our body. And every one who puts it on in
truth, by humility takes the likeness of Him that has
descended from His height. (1/LXXXII:384)

Only humility opens us to receptivity, reversing Adam's
pride and rejection of God: "To the humble the mysteries
are revealed" (1/LXXXII:388). Isaac is emphatic:

Humility of heart can occur in someone for two different reasons: either as a result of a precise knowledge
of one's sins; or as a result of recollecting the lowliness
of our Lord. . . . to what extent the greatness of the
Lord of all lowered itself in order to speak to and instruct us humans . . . abasing Himself to such an extent that He even took a body from humanity; how
much did our Lord's body endure, what did it have to
go through. (2/XVIII:6)

Down and Down . . .

Worship imparts such knowledge. The Orthodox liturgy
proclaims the *kenosis* or self-emptying in the descent of the
divine Word: "Hearken, O heaven, and give ear, O earth.
Let the foundations be shaken, and let trembling lay hold
upon the nethermost parts of the world. For our God and
Creator has clothed himself in created flesh . . . . O the
depth of the riches of the wisdom and knowledge of God!"[6]

Or as the Western antiphon for Christmas Eve puts it,
"For while all things were in quiet silence, and the night
was in the midst of her course, Thy almighty Word leapt
down from heaven from thy royal throne" (Wis 18:14, 15).

6. Mother Mary and Kallistos Ware, trans., *The Festal Menaion* (London:
Faber and Faber, 1969), 238.

In his passion, Christ penetrates the lowest parts of the earth, the underworld. He enters the captivities of human fear and despair, the most profound anxieties of humanity. The Apostles' Creed tells us, "He descended into hell." Jesus is buried in the depths of the earth, but in the mystery of Holy Saturday the work of redemption is being accomplished silently, secretly, in the darkness of the grave. Christ is busy in the underworld: "Christ was put to death in the flesh, but made alive in the spirit, in which also he went and made a proclamation to the spirits in prison" (1 Pet 3:18, 19). An Orthodox hymn sings the liberating truth:

> You descended to earth's depths,
> And smashed the eternal bars
> Which held the captives fast.[7]

An Anglican prayer for Morning Prayer puts it this way:

> Now, through the deep waters of death, you have brought your people to new birth by raising your Son to life in triumph. (*Common Worship*, Church of England)

Risk the Descent

The concept of depth is becoming more frequent in contemporary spirituality.[8] Paul Tillich in his groundbreaking study

---

7. Hugh Whybrew, *Risen with Christ* (London: SPCK, 2001), 28.

8. See, for example, Andrew D. Mayes, *Journey to the Centre of the Soul* (Abingdon: BRF, 2017); Yves Raguin, *The Depth of God* (Wheathampstead: Anthony Clarke Books, 1975); Mother Mary Clare, *Encountering the Depths* (London: Darton, Longman & Todd, 1981); William Clemmons, *Discovering the Depths: Guidance in Spiritual Growth* (London: Triangle / SPCK, 1989); Brother Ramon, *Deeper into God* (Basingstoke: Marshall Pickering, 1987).

The Shaking of the Foundations invited us to rediscover the metaphor of the depths of God:

> Most of our life continues on the surface. We are en-slaved by the routine of our daily lives . . . .We are in constant motion and never stop to plunge into the depth. We talk and talk and never listen to the voices speaking to our depth and from our depth . . . . It is comfortable to live on the surface . . . . It is painful to break away from it and to descend into an unknown ground.[9]

We are summoned to quit superficial living and risk a descent into the depths, where we may find God and in the process rediscover ourselves. Richard Foster writes, "Su-perficiality is the curse of our age . . . . The desperate need today is not for a greater number of intelligent people, or gifted people, but for deep people."[10] In his book *Contempla-tive Prayer*, Thomas Merton writes, "Monastic prayer begins not so much with 'considerations' as with a 'return to the heart,' finding one's deepest center, awakening the pro-found depths of our being." In another place he affirms, "The things on the surface are nothing, what is deep is the Real."[11] David Anderson writes,

> I love that image of God because it completely flips the dominant image of God "up there." When we first imagine a deity, God is always "up," always distant,

9. Paul Tillich, *The Shaking of the Foundation* (New York: Charles Scrib-ner & Sons, 1955), chap. 7.

10. Richard Foster, *Celebration of Discipline* (London: Harper, 1988), 1.

11. From an informal address delivered in Calcutta, India (October 1968); *The Asian Journal of Thomas Merton* (New York: New Directions, 1975), quoted in Lawrence S. Cunningham, ed., *Thomas Merton, Spiritual Master: The Essential Writings* (New York: Paulist Press, 1992), 237.

the Sky God of nearly every ancient religion. Until gradually it dawns upon us that the God whom the cosmos cannot contain is actually deep within. The ground of our being. And that underground river runs right through you. Sink a well within yourself and in the hidden darkness of your soul the river erupts. Water! Through the prophet God promises even "streams in the desert." God is the subterranean gusher and prayer is the well. Draw deeply—and often.[12]

Mystery and Revelation: The Spiritual Quest

> As God is elusive and invisible, thus also are His revelations. (3/IX:27)

We encounter a central paradox in prayer: God is both hidden and revealed, treasure buried and unearthed, concealed and exposed. At the same time, we come face to face with both mystery and revelation. Isaac affirms,

> The more the righteous advance to the vision of Him, the more they see an enigmatic sight. (1/XLV:217)

> examining, for the universal renovation, the secrets that were hidden in the mysterious silence of the Lord of the universe. (1/LXVI:316)

> There is nothing which grants the sublimity of love as the discovery of His love for us. There is nothing that lifts the mind in wonder, beyond all which is visible, to abide with Him far off from the worlds, as searching the mysteries of His nature. (3/I:16)

12. David Anderson, "God is an underground river," findingyoursoul .com/category/abundance/.

Isaac the Syrian, encouraging us to dive for pearls, invites us to view the Christian life as a search for the Divine, an ever-increasing openness and receptivity to God in prayer. Pearls are found only through dedicated searching. Isaac writes of our longings, "that first stirring consists in the power of the holy desire that is implanted in the soul's nature" (2/XVII:1). God plants within the soul a deep yearning desire that searches for the divine.

Uncovering Hidden Treasures

Two themes are interwoven in the Scriptures and in Isaac's writings. One is the theme of priceless treasures that we long for; the other is the perplexing yet enticing theme that God's treasures are both hidden and revealed.

Isaac writes that sometimes the treasures of "wonderful intuitions" may be stumbled upon in the course of prayer:

> The soul in its thoughts during ecstasy will desist from the use of the wonted deliberations—natural practice— by reason of the novel experiences which reach it from the sea of their mysteries. Even when the mind is floating on its upper waters, without being able to make its impulses deep as the depth of the waters (so that it can see all the treasures in its abysses)—still meditation, by its power of love, will have sufficient force to bind the thoughts firmly together with thoughts of ecstasy so that they are checked from thinking of and running after the nature of the body. (1/I:3)

> When the waters from without do not enter the fountain of the soul, its natural waters will arise, viz. the wonderful intuitions which are moving towards God at all times . . . when the senses are fenced in by solitude without a break . . . then thou wilt see what the nature of the deliberations of the soul, and what the nature of the soul is, and what treasures are collected

> in it. These treasures are incorporeal intuitions which
> arise from the soul without care or labor being spent
> on them. (1/III:14)

Isaac celebrates the role of the Holy Spirit in leading us
to revelation:

> When, then, prayer has come near to this place of reve-
> lation . . . this is called . . . knowledge of the myster-
> ies of the Spirit. When, indeed, the intellect [mind] is
> clothed with the Spirit, from that time it possesses . . .
> the knowledge of the Spirit, the reflection of the Spirit
> and the vision of the Spirit . . . it is brought from in-
> sight to insight. (3/IX:18)

> The one . . . who is directed towards hidden realities,
> remains in the Spirit. (3/IX:20)

> The revelations . . . which are made known by the Holy
> Spirit, lead to the knowledge of the future world . . . .
> Only the Spirit is able to make known this His mystery;
> He who by His power is prepared to give that greatest
> way of life which is beyond words. (3/IX:30, 31)

Seeing in the Dark

The mystic writers explore this theme through the image of
darkness, but as Melvyn Matthews cautions, this summons
us to a different mind-set and an expansion of our normal
patterns of thought: "We have become used to thinking of
the Christian faith in terms of the light that it provides, the
illumination that it gives to the mind and soul. To understand it as a step into darkness requires a different frame of
mind, a change of attitude for which we are little prepared."[13]

13. Melvyn Matthews, *Both Alike to Thee: The Retrieval of the Mystical
Way* (London: SPCK, 2000).

We are also summoned to discover fresh images of God. We are so used to thinking of a God up there or out there, a God remote enough not to disturb us! Sometimes this goes with Sunday School images of an old man with a beard or a judging schoolmaster god looking down on us with a scowl on his face. In a dualistic perspective that opposes the divine and human, God is seen as transcendent, beyond the world. But now we are invited to discover God within, below, beneath. As Matthew Fox puts it, "To relocate divinity in the depths of nature and of the self is to re-encourage an entire civilization to listen to its creative powers and to allow those powers to emerge once again. Divinity most emerges from the depths."[14]

Dionysius: Leave Everything Behind

Isaac seems to have encountered the influential fifth-century writer known as Dionysius, who summons us to the unfathomable depths of God:

> the mysteries of God's Word
> lie simple, absolute and unchangeable
> in the brilliant darkness of a hidden silence.
> Amid the deepest shadow
> they pour overwhelming light
> on what is most manifest.

> Amid the wholly unsensed and unseen
> they completely fill our sightless minds
>   with treasures beyond all beauty.[15]

---

14. Matthew Fox, *Wrestling with the Prophets* (1995; New York: Tarcher/Putnam, 2003), 13.

15. "The Mystical Theology," 1, in *Pseudo-Dionysius: The Complete Works*, trans. Colm Luibheid (New York: Paulist Press, 1987), 135. See also Andrew Louth, *Denys the Aeropagite* (London: Continuum, 1989).

As we plunge into that darkness that is beyond intellect, we find ourselves not simply running short of words but actually speechless and unknowing.[16] Andrew Louth explains, "It is an experience beyond the senses and beyond the intellect; it is a feeling awareness of a fragrance that delights and enraptures the soul."[17]

Dionysius entices us to the dark depths of the ocean:

> Leave behind you everything perceived and understood, everything perceptible and understandable, all that is not and all that is, and, with your understanding laid aside, strive . . . as much as you can toward union with him who is beyond all being and knowledge. By an undivided and absolute abandonment of yourself and everything, shedding all and freed from all, you will be uplifted to the ray of the divine shadow which is above everything that is.[18]

As Dionysius finds himself drawn irresistibly to a place of utter self-abandonment before the mystery of the Divine, so too Isaac longs that we decisively quit our safe spaces of prayer and dare to take a riskier path.

Divine Concealment and Disclosure in Isaac: Expect the Unexpected

Isaac wants to deliver us from predictable routine times of prayer marked by low expectation. He wants us to approach

---

16. Dionysius, "Mystical Theology," 139.

17. Andrew Louth, *The Origins of the Christian Mystical Tradition* (Oxford: Oxford University Press, 1981), 91. For a more cautious approach to mystical experience but celebrating the apophatic tradition in theology, see Denys Turner, *The Darkness of God: Negativity in Christian Mysticism* (Cambridge: Cambridge University Press, 1995).

18. Dionysius, "Mystical Theology," 135.

prayer with expectancy and a readiness for encountering the God of surprises. Insights and pearls discovered in prayer will always be a gift and a grace. What is required of us is utter openness. We come with thirst, longing, but do not predict what we will find. We do not attempt to squeeze divinity into the straitjackets formed through inherited ideas and practices. Let God be God! Be prepared for surprises, shock, awe, wonderment, falling silent . . . . Isaac distinguishes three different kinds of knowledge that we might gain:

> When knowledge pursues visible things, concerning which instruction is acquired through the senses, it is called natural.
> When it pursues the intelligible forces behind the visible things . . . it is called spiritual.
> When however knowledge pursues the Essence it is called supernatural, or rather agnostic . . . . by a sudden working of grace within, unexpectedly, it is revealed in the soul . . . . And it will not come from the place where it is expected, nor through observation, according to the word of our Lord [Luke 17:20]. But within the hidden form of the intellect it is revealed without cause and without meditation upon it. (1/LII:253)

Isaac writes often of this interplay between hiddenness and revelation:

> *in the stillness things come out into the open . . . they are perceived and recognized . . . .* The revelation of the good that is hidden within us is the apperception of knowledge of truth. The Kingdom of heaven is mystically within you . . . we call "truth" the right reflection on God which stems from Him, upon which someone stumbles in their mind, in a kind of state of wonder: amazing thoughts occur in the soul at the spiritual

stirrings concerning hidden matters—a wonder at
spiritual mysteries. (2/VIII:Title & 1)

Indeed, for Isaac, receiving revelations in the practice of
receptive prayer can be called "the sum of all contemplation," "heaven in the heart":

> There are people who taste of the mysteries of truth
> . . . . It is clear that if the heart can be worthy to be-
> come the location of heaven for the Lord, then it has
> been held worthy of the sum of all contemplation, with
> the vision of revelation. (2/XX:22, 23)

We can be prepared to receive wondrous revelations:

> place on your heart the contemplation of the mysteries
> of our Savior, for by this God will be revealed to you
> in wondrous revelations . . . in a silent form of reve-
> lation and in visionless insights there is revealed to
> this abode, in the inner sanctuary of the heart, a reve-
> lation concerning the mystery of knowledge of Him.
> (2/XLI:2)

Into the Deepest, Darkest Waters of Prayer

Isaac's writings celebrate the enigmatic workings of God,
his hidden purposes, often unfathomable and unsearchable.
As we shall see, when Isaac leads us into the "Beyond,"
from pure prayer to spiritual prayer, we are beginning to
tread the *via negativa*, the apophatic path of unknowing.
Here in the darkest, deepest waters of prayer, we realize
that God is always beyond our best concepts and categories,
and human language cannot communicate his wonder. We
move beyond words to the prayer of dumbfounded amazement. We come to the point where we admit the limits of
our language when attempting to speak of God. Isaiah confesses, "Truly, you are a God who hides himself" (Isa 45:15).

With Paul we say, "O the depth of the riches and wisdom and knowledge of God! How unsearchable are his judgments and how inscrutable his ways!" (Rom 11:33).

Isaac quotes with approval the words of Evagrius: "Blessed is he who has reached, during prayer, unconsciousness which is not to be surpassed" (1/XXII:118). Echoing language of Gregory of Nyssa and Pseudo-Dionysius, Isaac states, "And though he [the seeker] has penetrated into the mysteries of all spiritual kinds (of beings) and possesses great wisdom concerning all the creatures, he knows with perfect certainty that he knows nothing" (1/LXXXII:387). Isaac uses the imagery beloved of the apophatic mystics: the "dark cloud" and the divine "darkness" (1/II:9). He observes, "And if thou findest that thy spirit, from time to time, descends . . . without unusual efforts, and abides there some time . . . then know that the cloud has begun to cover the tabernacle" (1/LXIX:322). He testifies to God of "the great thick darkness which surrounds Your holiness . . . the secret place of the thick darkness of Your glory" (3/VII:7). Isaac longs to guide us to the place of deepest silence in the ocean of God's love, where an unspeakable perception of God's mysteries is characterized by an amazement beyond words.

Seeking Vision

Nevertheless Isaac urges us to develop our faculties and enlarge our capacity for the discovery of the Divine in times of prayer, opening wide our spiritual eyes:

> Vision of the mind, I call revelation of hidden things, and the understanding of incorporeal things, and that certain understanding which is given by the Spirit. (3/IX:5)

Isaac reassures us that true vision is indeed possible:

> There is the true vision of that in which consists our
> Kingdom and our glory. (3/III:33)

> The true vision of Jesus Christ our Lord consists in our
> realizing the meaning of His dispensation for our
> sakes, and becoming inebriated with love of Him as a
> result of the insights into the many wondrous elements
> contained in that vision. (2/XIV:30)

As we progress, we find ourselves echoing the heart-felt
prayer of Isaac:

> May God perfect us with knowledge of His mysteries,
> forever and ever, amen. (2/XV:11)

It is to this search and to these revelations in prayer that
we shortly turn.

Questions for Reflection

1. To which image of the spiritual life are you most naturally drawn—the ascent or the descent? Why?

2. Why do you think the descent model has been less attractive or less utilized in the history of Christian spirituality?

3. How does the theme of mystery and revelation play out
   in your life? What key things have you discovered about
   the nature of prayer? What would you describe as *mystery*? How comfortable are you about living with this
   paradox?

4. Why do you think Jesus is sometimes insistent about secrecy? Recall Christ's teaching on the hiddenness of true prayer in the Sermon on the Mount: "When you pray, go into your private room, shut the door, and pray to your Father in that secret place" (Matt 6:6). (The Greek word used for *secret* here is *kruptos,* denoting something hidden or concealed.)

5. What is your experience of receiving insight or revelation from the Holy Spirit? How can you tell that this has happened?

6. How do you find yourself responding to the idea that God might be found in deep darkness? What do you make of Melvyn Matthews's observation: "To understand [the Christian faith] as a step into darkness requires a different frame of mind, a change of attitude for which we are little prepared"?

Prayer Exercise

Take time to make a personal refection on the themes of this chapter. Standing in imagination before a newly plowed field or standing at the edge of shimmering blue waters, wonder to yourself what might lurk below the surface, waiting to be discovered. What, spiritually speaking, would you love to see emerging from the hidden depths? What grace of insight do you yearn for?

Surrender these to God. Pray for the grace of determination and utter openness to what God has in store for you. And give thanks.

5. FACING THE CURRENTS

Pour forth Your peace on our hearts
and Your calm on our stirrings. (3/X:33)

What bubbles to the surface when you come to pray? In this chapter we see what Isaac teaches about currents in the ocean of the soul that he calls "stirrings." As he puts it, "We will begin by distinguishing the stirrings of human knowledge, both the level below the nature of the soul, and the upsurges which are supernatural" (2/XX:1). We see here how refreshing and honest Isaac is in describing the experience of prayer, taking into account our sometimes conflicting feelings: he emerges as both a realist and an optimist.

Though Isaac does not directly liken the stirrings to underwater currents, he uses dynamic watery language to describe them: "*surging* of grace," "*gushing forth* in their impetus" (2/XXXII:1); "*upsurges* which are supernatural" (2/XX:1); "the mind finds itself above the world in its *upsurge*" (2/XXXIV:2). He writes, "knowledge of truth *plunges* us out of contests and reflection on them, and *mingles* us with our stirrings with God" (2/X:16). He writes of a brief "stirring which *wells up* in the mind" (2/III:4, 66). He delights in "the *flow* of His grace" (2/XXXIX:2). "Sometimes charisms that are partial occur during prayer, such as a profusion of tears, or a delight at the words of the prayer *welling up* in the heart . . . or a *bubbling up* of thanksgiving . . . or it may be a sudden stirring of hope during prayer"

81

(2/XIV:27). Isaac writes, "the mind has been *engulfed* by the divine Spirit" (1/XXII:115). "The *flood* of Christ's mysteries presses upon my mind like the waves of the sea" (2/V:19). He writes of those "*submerged* into silence" (2/V:1).

Isaac says that if there is no bubbling up of stirrings that touch on the divine Name, we can't really talk of the love of God: "I am amazed if there is anyone in whom these stirrings concerning that divine Name do not bubble up who claims to know what the love of God is" (2/X:29). He writes of "inner turbulence" (2/XXI:5) evoking swirling currents in the soul. There is the experience too of outer turbulence: "The stirring of the sea of the body through the impulses which agitate it against the ship of the mind" (1/XXXVIII:195). In this chapter we develop the heuristic potential of a metaphor—we explore its suggestions and take forward its hints as we consider the currents that become manifest in prayer. We seek "a mind made mature in the stirrings which partake of the divine outpouring" (2/XL:4).

Stirrings Human and Divine

In the course of prayer, we will experience diverse currents or flows of thought. The mind and the soul will experience fluctuations, motions, and indeed we will experience prayer shifts and changes in our thinking. We will find ourselves vacillating in attitudes and responses to the outer world. Sometimes undercurrents—representing things we may be denying or burying, aspects of our shadow side—might break into consciousness.

First to bubble up within us, as we come before God in prayer, will be very human stirrings. These might include our aspirations, our hopes and dreams, our longings, yearnings, deepest desires. They might encompass our anxieties and fears, or feelings of penitence or regret.

Isaac writes of the need for the mind to "cling to those impulses which are interwoven with prayer" (1/LXIII:296). He is clear: "It is not possible for a man to come near to Christ without troubles" (1/XXXV:153). Arent Wensinck comments, "It may be added here that the terms impulses, emotions, though often used in a sense similar to that of affections, cover a much wider field . . . . they denote the whole activity of the invisible part of man, and a single time even the phrase 'emotions of the body' occurs."

In prayer, a complexity of thoughts gradually surges to the surface of consciousness. We experience in the ocean of the soul a maelstrom of swirling hopes and desires. The soul becomes a vortex, a whirlpool, as competing dreams and fears eddy within us, fed by both passions and grace:

> Examine thyself constantly, my beloved, and pay attention to the steadfastness of thy labors, and the troubles assailing thee . . . the frequent drogues of temptations that are continually administered by the true physician in order to heal the inner man; sometimes however by the demons. Sometimes they come through illnesses or bodily sufferings, sometimes through the terrors of the emotions of thy soul . . . . Sometimes through the tenderness and fostering of grace there will arise warmth and sweet tears and spiritual joy and all the other things. (1/LXX:324)

Evagrius of Pontus had taught in his *Praktikos* that it is possible to discern the origin of *logismoi* or tempting thoughts by observing their effects at an emotional level—a state of disturbance might point to demonic sources, for example. A millennium later, Ignatius of Loyola was to develop subtle teaching on discernment, reflecting on consolations and desolations and tracing the origin and effects of feelings. But we are not to read Isaac through Ignatian eyes. As we noted in chapter two, Isaac speaks of gaining luminosity or illumination about the swirling currents we experience. He alerts us both to the ever-present pull of this world, with its lure of attachment, and to the reality that the Holy Spirit is powerfully at work in our lives—we could say, like a powerful life-giving Gulf Stream drawing into its transformative flow our turbulent waters. The Holy Spirit gives us, as we know, "love, joy, peace, patience, kindness, generosity, faithfulness, gentleness, and self-control" (Gal 5:22, 23); to these, we might add courage, compassion, humility, hope. Isaac celebrates the movement of the Holy Spirit in the soul:

> this is an indication of the mysteries and the perfect knowledge which the saints receive mingled into their prayers, through the wisdom of the Spirit. (2/XIV:43)

> The flood of Christ's mysteries presses upon my mind like the waves of the sea . . . . O sinner, . . . it is by meditating upon this that the mud of sin will be shaken off your mind. (2/V:19)

Confluence of Currents

A mingling of the waters takes place as different elements meet and interpenetrate, a convergence between the priorities of our human spirit and those of the Divine Spirit. Which will win out, the springing up of the Divine Spirit, or human emotions and concerns? Prayer is a confluence and an interaction, a synergy in which we do our part and God does his part in prayer. Paul explains that when we find ourselves crying out to God as Abba Father,

> It is that very Spirit bearing witness with our spirit that we are children of God. (Rom 8:16, NRSV)

> For the Spirit himself joins with our spirits. Together they tell us that we are God's children. The Holy Spirit makes

God's fatherhood real to us as he whispers into our innermost being, "You are God's beloved child!" (Rom 8:16, The Passion Translation)

Isaac writes, "While he is fully in the mode of life of the soul, every now and then it happens that some stirrings of the spirit arise indistinctly in him, and he begins to perceive in his soul a hidden joy and consolation: like flashes of lightening . . . particular mystical insights arise and are set in motion in his mind. At this his heart bursts with joy" (2/XX:19, 20).

In the natural world, places where ocean currents collide can be both treacherous and fruitful. Areas where warm and cold currents meet produce regular foggy conditions when overlying warm and cold air come in contact with each other, but they also have high biological productivity, because the mixing of warm and cold currents encourages plankton growth. Some of the world's most productive areas for fishing are located where warm and cold currents converge. Off the coast of Newfoundland, the fresh icy Labrador Current from the Arctic encounters the warm salty waters of the Gulf Stream. While the water is shrouded in dense fog on the surface, beneath the surface life flourishes as one of the richest fishing grounds of the world. The two water masses have different densities, so they don't blend seamlessly into each other, but collide. Like low and high pressure air masses in the atmosphere above them, these water masses form fronts or boundaries, which continually interact and move in response to passing weather systems. The shifting of these oceanic fronts creates the equivalent of weather within the ocean. They stir up nutrients from the deep that benefit fish and marine mammals. The natural world seems to mirror and reflect the inner:

When it sometimes happens that a person is held worthy of prayer of fervor as a result of the surging of grace, then he experiences countless densely-packed stirrings in this prayer: prayers press on each other in a forceful way, prayers both pure and hot . . . . In the midst of these stirrings a mighty gasp ascends from the depths of the heart . . . . he receives a hidden assistance in his stirrings at these times from the prayer itself . . . . that person is lowered to the abyss in his thoughts. Thus these stirrings issue forth for him in his prayer in the form of pure and forceful prayers, densely-packed and gushing forth in their impetus: they are in the most inmost part of the heart, and are accompanied by an unswerving gaze directed towards our Lord. It seems to that person that it is in his very body that he is approaching our Lord at that time, because of the sincerity of the prayer's thoughts which rise up for him. (2/XXXII:1)

What Is Happening in this Meeting of the Currents?

Isaac identifies various processes that take place within this interaction. As we open ourselves to the divine light and allow rays of sunlight, as it were, to penetrate into our murky mixed-up waters of prayer, our minds and thinking receive the grace to see things more clearly—we receive the gift of luminosity in our thoughts. Isaac delights in the idea of luminosity—as more and more divine light filters through our thinking, we will experience different degrees of transformation. We will see things in greater clarity: "When the Spirit shines out in our hearts, then the movements of our meditation . . . are brought close to luminosity; then our intellect, not through any act of will on its part, is drawn up, by means of some kind of reflection, in wonder towards God" (2/X:2).

Isaac encourages a process of clarification and discernment when he talks about such illumination:

And it is becoming that thou arousest thyself and with
tears beseechest the Saviour of the world that He may
take away the veil from the heart, and disperse from
the inner firmament the darkness of the clouds of the
affections; and that thou mayest be deemed worthy of
seeing the rays of daylight. (1/LXX:327)

Sometimes we can see things from God's point of view.
There is a process of purifying our thoughts and a greater
sense of illumination:

Just as purity of heart . . . is not a matter of someone
being totally without thought or reflection or stirring,
but rather it consists in the heart being purified of all
evil, and in gazing favorably on everything, and consid-
ering it from God's point of view, so it is the same with
pure and undistracted prayer. (2/XV:2; see also 2/XXI:2)

Grace shifts our perceptions during prayer. As in the
Psalms, we realize not only that it is good and healthy to
express our human stirrings and questions to God, but also
that expressing them may enable their transformation. For
example, Psalms 22 and 42 begin with despair but move,
step by step, to trust and hope. Isaac testifies to such a transformational character of prayer. We gradually learn to re-
focus our thoughts in prayer in a Godward orientation. Isaac
tells us that if we just dwell on human stirrings and issues,
we will not get very far—we might get stuck, fixated: "such
a person just concentrates on matters of the passions"
(2/X:7). But there is a better way: "But if he meditates on
God and allows his mind to wander on the things that be-
long to Him, searching God out single-mindedly, then he
will be illumined" (2/X:8). Isaac explains:

Once the intellect is engaged in meditating on God it is
raised above contest. It is not that it actually vanquishes

the thoughts, stirrings and passions, but it reigns over
them, and they vanish away . . . . once someone meditates on God and on the riches of the waves of everything that belongs to Him and applies to Him, then he
has departed from the world. (2/X:13)

Isaac commends a letting go and a certain detachment,
for this requires of us a resolve, discipline, and determination, not to give into human stirrings but to learn the art of
recollecting the mind's thoughts, re-rooting them in God,
refocusing on God—a reorientation of our thinking:

It is in proportion to the honor which someone shows
in his person to God during the time of prayer, both
with his body and with the mind, that the door of assistance will be opened for him, leading to the purifying of the impulses and to illumination in prayer.
(2/XIV:11)

The Paradoxes of Prayer

In his desert experience Jesus found the wilderness to be a
place of angels and demons: "He was in the wilderness for
forty days, tempted by Satan; and he was with the wild
beasts; and the angels waited on him" (Mark 1:13). Isaac
tells us that in the waters of prayer we will encounter both
reassuring dolphins[19] and threatening sharks (2/XXXIV:4).

In today's world, we are alert to both nutrients and toxins
found in the ocean's waters. Isaac helpfully tells us that we
are likely in prayer to experience a "variation between assistance and feebleness." He testifies to the ways in which
we may feel an upsurge of confidence and affirmation, di-

19. 1/15:85, trans. Miller.

vinely given, then find ourselves plunging into a sense of desolation and awareness of our human fragility:

> Thus in this way the variation between assistance and feebleness takes place for a person at all times and at all stages in the ascetic life: it may be in the battles waged against chastity, or in the varied states of joy and gloom; for sometimes there are luminous and joyous stirrings, but then again all at once there is darkness and cloud. Likewise with the things revealed in certain mystical and divine insights concerning truth: the same variation is experienced by the person who serves God, with the apperception of the assistance of divine power that suddenly attaches itself to the intellect. Or it may be the apperception of the opposite, where the intention is that he should receive awareness of the weakness of human nature, and realize what his own nature is, and how weak. (2/IX:11)

The inbreaking of these perceptions may be both unbidden and irresistible—the spontaneity of grace:

> On occasion the suffering and pain of his heart will cause all sorts of deeply-felt words of prayer to spring up, or joy may burst forth in response to something, stirring that person to alter his prayer to praises owing to the delight his mind feels. The same applies to other stirrings at prayer which the Holy Spirit sets in motion in the saints, in whose utterances are ineffable mysteries and insights. (2/XIV:43)

The spiritual seeker must uphold a certain intentionality in order to remain open to God's inflowing graces and insights:

> You are wise enough not to require of the mind motionlessness—as do the fools; for this cannot be asked

of human nature. Rather strive to discover stirrings that
are good during the time of prayer, as the wise do.
These consist in: reflection on the Spirit's insights, and
a sagacious purpose which considers during the time
of prayer how to please the will of the Maker of all: this
is the final end of all virtue and of all prayer. (2/XV:10)

Wanderings

Allowing our thoughts to wander in prayer can be good as
long as they become increasingly God-directed. We are not
to concentrate on bad or empty thoughts, but rather leave
these behind. Isaac encourages us to be explorers and to
allow our thoughts to wander creatively, expectantly, and
searchingly. Isaac uses words like *search, discover*: "finding
that for which you yearn without being aware of it, namely,
the apperception of God, the wonderment of mind that is
free of all images, and the spiritual silence of which the
Fathers speak" (2/XV:11). He speaks of wandering in a
sense of roaming playfully and curiously and inquisitively,
seeking God amid the cloudy waters of prayer:

> For there is a good kind of wandering and a bad kind
> of wandering. When you are in prayer, do not seek to
> be entirely free of mental wandering, which is impos-
> sible, but seek to wander following something that is
> good. . . . Wandering is bad when someone is dis-
> tracted by empty thoughts or by reflecting on some-
> thing bad. . . . Wandering is good when the mind
> wanders on God during the entire extent of its prayer,
> on His glory and majesty, stemming from a recollection
> of the Scriptures, and at insights into the divine utter-
> ances and holy words of the Spirit. (2/XV:3–5)

So, Isaac says, don't think for a minute that wanderings
are wrong. It is a question of their starting points and of the
direction they take you in:

> For we do not consider as alien to purity of prayer and
> as detrimental to collectedness of thoughts in prayer
> any profitable recollections that may spring up in the
> mind from the writings of the Spirit, resulting in in-
> sights and spiritual understanding of the divine world
> during the time of prayer. (2/XV:5)

As currents and stirrings rise within us we will vacillate:
as Isaac discovered as a writer, sometimes we think of
heaven, then of earth, we move between wonder at creation
and anxiety at suffering, between physical concerns and
hidden spiritual meanings (2/XXXVI).

Jesus' forty-day sojourn in the desert was not only a time
of temptation and trial but a hugely formative and creative
experience for him. As he learned to listen ever more at-
tentively to his Father's voice, he discerned and clarified
his priorities: he saw what was important and what was
not. He emerged from this time strengthened and with a
clear sense of his mission, ready to announce his greatest
goal: "The Kingdom of God has come near" (Mark 1:14).
As Isaac also discovered, struggle with conflicting currents
of passions and desires can lead to discernment and fresh
resolve, a greater openness to God's future.

Questions for Reflection

1. Which stirrings in your soul do you find most challenging? What movements or shifts do you detect in yourself
   when you come to prayer?

2. How do you distinguish between stirrings human and
   divine within you?

3. What is your experience of a confluence of such currents in your soul? Which wins out, if any?

4. What is your experience of "dolphins and sharks" in the waters of your soul? What positive and creative things might emerge from such a struggle, from such ripples in the soul?

Prayer Exercise

Place yourself slowly and deliberately in the presence of God. Become aware of your body, any restlessness, any longings of soul.

As you come to prayer, what is stirring within you? What is bubbling up? What is rising to the surface from the depths? Take stock.

Give name to your stirrings. Begin with the very human ones. Acknowledge each of them and do not try to suppress them. Rather, express them in prayer before God.

Can you notice in yourself any stirrings that might be divine in origin, God-given? Desires in the soul that resonate strongly with the Gospel? Name them. Celebrate them. Give thanks for each of them.

Pray that they might strengthen and intermingle with the human stirrings, gradually transforming them. Rest within this interaction and interpenetration between the human and the Divine.

Or

To prepare for our next chapter, Isaac's three stages of prayer, undertake a sinking exercise. Picture yourself and imagine yourself descending in a gentle sea of grace.

1. Body awareness: become aware of the depth or shallowness of your breathing, tension or relaxation in your limbs, your heart rate.

2. Soul stirrings: Be true to yourself as you come before God in utter honesty—lower any self-defensive barriers or shields you may deliberately or inadvertently erect before God. Picture them moving down, or crumbling away, until you come to a place of vulnerability and utter openness before the Divine. Begin to enter into your feelings and responses before God. Give name to them. What is happening?

3. Spirit silence: Allow yourself to sink deeper. Let go of the stirrings; release them as a diver, as it were, might release his or her grip on a piece of wood carried far below. See the stirrings floating up and away. Permit yourself to sink into a place of deep stillness. Become as receptive as you can, expectant, listening, waiting, longing.

Be careful to bring to a close the prayer exercise with an act of reflection, thanksgiving, and conclusion, so you can return gently, as it were, to the surface.

6. Embracing Transitions

immerse my soul in the deepest depths of quiet in God.
(1/LXVI:314)

Isaac is leading us toward a place of stillness where stirrings and turbulence are left behind. We move, as it were, toward the ocean floor, and it is here that prayer learns to be receptive to the Divine. We see how Isaac opens up for us a spiritual itinerary or journey marked by three broad stages, and we note what he says about transitioning among them.

Although Isaac never presents a systematic theory of prayer, he very clearly identifies three levels of prayer. Isaac celebrates a sense of progression. We begin with verbalizing prayer through the use of psalms and other liturgical prayers. As we go deeper we encounter the stirrings in the soul, human and divine. This stage is characterized by prayers of active meditation. But we are summoned to the depths, to wordless contemplation, where we become more receptive than ever to divinely given insights. It is a movement: the practice of prayer "sets in motion the state of being fully alive" (3/IX:17). Chapter XX of the Second Part is a key passage about the different levels. Isaac is following John of Apamea in this version of the "triple way." His teaching can be understood as successive stages on a journey of increasing maturity and openness to God, or as three different levels of perception—three degrees of knowledge.[1]

---

1. As explored in Part 1 (1/LI:248–53).

The Level of the Body

Stirrings on the level of the body concern physical concerns and worries: "he thinks of the things of the body" (2/XX:13). We are acutely aware of our mortality, our physical needs and passions. From time to time fear of death surfaces:

> Prayer is the place of the soul where the fulfillment of the bodily way of life occurs. The way of life is from the working of the body: fasting, the Office, alms, labors, chastity, service to the sick, silence, weeping, obedience, renunciation, mercy. . . . These ways are the limit for bodily activity. Prayer, however, is the contemplation of the soul . . . more profound than what can be examined. (3/IX:1, 2)

This initial phase of the spiritual journey is characterized by the rhythms and routines of the Daily Office and by verbalized, audible expressions of prayer. At the beginning of the journey, there is a single path and a single beginning for all who travel in stillness: psalms, fasting, Scripture reading (2/XXXI:1, 2). Gradually through prayer and spiritual reading there is a "deepening and progression from insight to what follows which is amazing and more luminous" (3/IX:5). We may find ourselves passing into a transitional stage, "where someone has in his manner of life and in his understanding left the level of the body, but has not yet fully entered the level of the soul . . . . As a result thoughts spring up in him coming from both sides" (2/XX:17).

The Level of the Soul

This stage is characterized by "stirrings on the level of the soul" (2/XXXII:6). As we sink deeper we leave surface thoughts and noise behind because "the revelations of the Holy Spirit are in silence" (3/IX:26). We begin to leave behind petitionary prayer and move toward the perfection of love:

Authentic prayer is the perception of what is in God. This is that prayer in which the mind abides not by means of petitions but by the perfection of love; and one remains in prayer before God not to ask for something or other, but to behold His Essence. (3/IV:1)

The perfection of love is more exalted than prayer stirred by requests. . . . The perfection of love . . . has no need to ask for anything other than the mind's contemplating God, insatiably. When indeed the mind enters into love and divine knowledge, it does not desire to present a petition for something or other, not even for what is elevated and very honorable. Prayer, then, of petitions and requests is an array of stirrings and prayers for contingencies, while the gift of love in prayer is the silence of the spirit. For when the mind is united to God, it desists from petition and prayer. (3/IV:1, 5–7)

Petitions fade away, making room and space, as it were, to receive from God insights and revelations:

Indeed, all one's desire [in respect to petitions] grows dim. By means of revelation and instead of all that, the knowledge of the Spirit fills one with those hidden realities by the revelation of insight . . . . This is his prayer: only to marvel at God . . . this gift of the Spirit continually shows him ineffable realities by means of insight, and in an inexplicable mystery. The instruction about hidden realities is imprinted on the mind, by means of the force of the Spirit. (3/IV:21, 22)

While maintaining spiritual disciplines of reading and meditation, we move toward receptive prayer. The liminal, transitional stage between the level of soul and the level of spirit becomes increasingly creative: "while he is fully in the mode of life of the soul, every now and then it happens that some stirrings of the spirit arise indistinctly in him, and he begins to perceive in his soul a hidden joy and consolation"

(2/XX:19). Mystical insights may come like lightning flashes. There can be no rigid demarcations between stages, but rather overlaps and, it is hoped, a sense of progression and going deeper.

The Level of the Spirit: Sink into Stillness

> *On the level and in the life of the spirit . . . [human nature]*
> *remains in a certain and inexplicable silence, for the working*
> *of the Holy Spirit stirs in it, it being raised above the realm*
> *of the soul's understanding.* (2/XXXII:4)

Isaac encourages us to sink deeper in our prayers—the deeper we go, the more we advance toward stillness and leave the eddies behind. We are summoned to a depth of stillness beyond stirrings and movements, resting in God in inexplicable stillness, anticipating the Life of the Age to Come: "he stands in the knowledge and joy which is in God, seeing that he has become a son and sharer in the mystery of God" (2/XX:15).

Here Isaac distinguishes between pure prayer and spiritual prayer. The difference between these is that during pure prayer one's mind brims with stirrings (*zaw'e*), while spiritual prayer does not entail any movement of the mind. Words give way to wonder. Spiritual prayer is the place of deep stillness. It is "The Beyond."

Cross Limits and Boundaries: Into the Beyond

Isaac wants to lead us across boundaries and beyond limits:

> all kinds and habits of prayer which mankind prays
> unto God, have their term [terminate] in pure prayer.
> Lamentations and self-humiliations and beseechings
> and inner supplications and sweet tears and all other
> habits which prayer possesses . . . their boundary and

the domain within which they are set in motion, is pure
prayer. (1/XXII:112)

He does not want us to be content with where we are,
but descend to the riskier depths of spiritual prayer. Paradoxically, he says this is, in a sense, not prayer at all, if we
are used to defining prayer as the expression of our needs
and hopes. We have left that behind:

> As soon as the spirit has crossed the boundary of pure
> prayer and proceeded onwards, there is neither prayer,
> nor emotions, nor tears . . . nor beseechings, nor de-
> sire, nor longing after any of those things which are
> hoped for in this world or in the world to be. Therefore
> there is no prayer beyond pure prayer, . . . but beyond
> this limit [the spirit] passes into ecstasy. (1/XXII:112)

The latter word is best translated "awestruck wonder."
We are beckoned to leave behind words and prayers and
sink deeper into a wordless communion with the Divine—a
sense of being at one with God. Words are no longer needed.
They become utterly redundant.

Enter "the Deepest Depths of Quiet in God"

On the surface of the ocean we experience turbulence with
large waves crashing and foaming. Beneath the surface currents and streams of water compete. But go down diving a
few hundred feet and it will be strangely quiet and calm
with serene fish swimming along. When oceanographer
Jacques Cousteau made his pioneering documentary of
underwater aquatic habitats in 1956 he entitled it *The Silent
World*. Greater treasures lie on the ocean floor. In Asia, some
pearl oysters can be found at a depth of five to seven feet
from the surface, but more often divers go 40 feet or even

up to 125 feet deep to find enough pearl oysters. These deep dives are at once risky and rewarding.

The deeper we go in prayer the more silent it becomes. We allow ourselves to sink in the ocean of grace. We leave behind the chaos and confusion, as we noted:

> Just as the dolphin stirs and swims about when the visible sea is still and calm, so also, when the sea of the heart is tranquil and still from wrath and anger, mysteries and divine revelations are stirred in her at all times to delight her. [2]

"The deepest depths of quiet in God": Isaac uses this phrase in Part 1, where he is reflecting on the three interlinked realities of solitude, silence, and stillness:

> When by prolonged solitude my heart has acquired peace from the trouble of recollections, solitude sends me continually waves of gladness which arise from emotions which burst forth from within unexpectedly and suddenly, to the delight of my heart; the which, running against the ship of my soul and withdrawing it from the sounds of the world [temptations] and from the life of the flesh, immerse it in the deepest depths of quiet in God. (1/LXVI:314)

Isaac recalls how Jesus himself models a pattern of withdrawal, detachment, and stillness:

> The Savior . . . honored and loved stillness at all times, saying "Let us go to the wilderness to rest by ourselves" and "He sat down in a boat and went to a deserted region with his disciples." It was especially

---

2. 1/15:85, trans. Miller.

at these times that He drew Himself away from people and remained in stillness . . . . For the instruction of the children of light who would travel afterwards in His footsteps following this new mode of life, He carried out this solitary converse with God. (2/XII:1)

We too can enjoy such encounters with God:

> A person who has stillness and the converse of knowledge will easily and quickly arrive at the love of God, and with the love of God he will draw close to perfect love of fellow human beings . . . we should leave the open space of struggles and give ourselves over to stillness. (2/X:33, 37)

But Isaac is emphatic that it takes great discipline, over both the tongue and the fluttering mind, to reach this place of quietude:

> There cannot be recollection of mind and purity in prayer without much vigilance over speech and action, as well as a guard over the senses; nor can the awareness that is given by grace come about unless a person has acquired much discernment by means of stillness. (2/XIV:10)

> Let us rejoice, then, and give thanks to God that we have been held worthy, even for a small moment, to be able to escape from chatter and talk with the passions—for we are, albeit just for one moment, through converse with some excellent meditation . . . this cannot be acquired without the continual reading of Scripture in stillness and the reflective search for things hidden, and prayer. (2/XXIX:4)

Hilarion Alfeyev raises important questions about the silence to which Isaac summons us:

> Is this complete cessation of the intellectual activity which Isaac calls stillness of mind not a sort of Buddhist Nirvana, a migration beyond the borders of every personal existence, a full loss of personal self-consciousness? The answer must be negative. In Isaac, stillness of mind is not a synonym for unconscious and insensible oblivion: there is a positive element in Isaac's stillness, the capture of the mind by God. Unlike Nirvana, stillness of mind is an extremely intense state of the mind, which finds itself entirely under the power of God and is drawn into undiscovered depths of the Spirit. The question concerns, therefore, the absence of the movements and desires of the intellect, but not the loss of personal existence: on the contrary, in the stillness of mind there is an intense personal communion of a human person with personal God. Spiritual prayer, which begins beyond the borders of pure prayer, is the descent of mind to a state of peace and stillness.[3]

One thing is sure: such silence is indispensable: "If someone does not have stillness, he will not come to know any one of these things [about God's love]" (2/XVIII:16). With Isaac may we exult: "after such insights, who will not laud you, O stillness, that harbor of mercies?" (2/XVIII:19).

Isaac encourages us to "dive into the sea of stillness" (2/XXXIV:5). Are you ready to make that further descent? Let's go for it!

---

3. Hilarion Alfeyev, "Prayer in St Isaac of Nineveh," paper delivered at the Conference on Prayer and Spirituality in the Early Church, Melbourne, Australia, August 1995.

Questions for Reflection

1. Broadly speaking, where would you locate yourself on Isaac's version of the three stages? How does your experience resonate with Isaac's three-part itinerary of the soul?

2. In your own terms, how would you describe the stage or phase you have reached on your spiritual journey? What clues or indicators do you notice and detect in yourself that might suggest that you are ready to go deeper? Is there evidence of a holy listlessness and desire for something more?

3. What is your experience of transition in the spiritual journey—leaving one phase of spiritual experience behind and entering upon another? How would you describe the necessity of "letting go"?

4. Why do you think deep silence is hard to discover even in our own spiritual lives? What would help? What hinders?

5. What expectancy do you have in your heart as you come to prayer? What do you think might happen in you if you came with greater openness and hopefulness?

Extended Prayer Exercise

In your imagination, stand on the gangplank of your ship or vessel. Look down at the surface of the sea. Is it calm or disturbed? The depths summon you, like an irresistible magnet drawing you in.

Adrenaline courses through your veins, and hope quickens your heartbeat. You sense you might be on the brink of a great discovery. You experience a kind of spiritual vertigo, feeling you might plummet into the darkness below at any moment. You are initially aghast at the chasms below: an eerie, inky blackness. From this angle, at the surface, you can't make anything out. It is awesome, fearful yet strangely inviting.

Dare you take a leap in the dark and dive far below? Can you let go of your grip and allow yourself to tumble? A sense of suspense dawns in your pounding heart. Are you ready for astonishing discoveries of God, which will be impossible to put into words? Are you prepared to become awestruck, dumbfounded, as you sink through Isaac's three levels?

Your heart is aquiver with a sense of anticipation and a little apprehension. Name your fears. Expel them—breathe them out. Deliberately give them over to God. Now is the time to leave behind verbalized prayers and petitions. It is time to quit thinking about your bodily needs. It is time to release all attachments and anything that holds you back or preoccupies your thinking with physical concerns.

There is no turning back. This is your moment! Let go, and Let God!

The time has come and you can't put off this moment any longer. You become decisive. Yes, I will quit my comfort zone. I will take the plunge!

You step out, and after a great splash you immerse yourself, submerge yourself, beneath the waters. You have no worries, as you are fully equipped, and prayer gives oxygen to the soul! You can breathe deeply. There is no danger of drowning. You will be safe. God inspires you—this literally means "breathes into" you.

You allow the stirrings in your soul to bubble up and away to the surface. Anxieties still want to challenge and distract you, but you let them pass. You may feel buffeted by currents, but this does not perturb you. Some currents—divine stirrings?—seem to strangely caress and reassure you.

As you permit yourself to descend, feel yourself surrounded and upheld by the warm cleansing waters of grace. Let the reality of God's love and compassion envelop you, embrace you, inundate your soul.

Notice the play of light, rays streaming from the sun being refracted through the waters. Down you go, the movement of the flippers on your feet propelling you. You look to right and left, and maybe see rocks. Maybe you catch sight of astonishing coral formations and find yourself amazed by their colors and intricacies. Shoals of multicolored fish pass you by. Look beneath you, and you see a wide inviting chasm and abyss. Allow yourself to sink down, down, down. You are soon approaching the ocean floor or shelf. It seems to be getting darker, and you experience a deep silence. It is not threatening but strangely rejuvenating, energizing.

What can you see now? What are you noticing? How do you feel right now? Explore with your fingertips different surfaces. Be prepared for a little digging. What can you unearth? What textures can you feel? What shapes can you make out? Be curious and inquisitive. Lift up rocks to see what you can find underneath.

What are you longing for with all your heart in your relationship with God, and with others? What is your heart's desire? What do you need right now? Name your longings before God (reassurance, guidance, forgiveness?).

You wonder to yourself: What might God surprise me with? What might delight my soul? A fresh call, a new grace?

Your eye is drawn to a cluster of oysters on the seabed. They really don't look very appealing or attractive on the outside, and some seaweed is cloaking them. But what awaits? Take one in your hand. Use a penknife to gently prize it open. What can you see?

There is a milky substance, but no pearl to be found. Reverently place it back on the seabed. Its time will come. It is not quite ready to embrace the mysterious process of forming a pearl from a piece of grit. The grit may be there, sure enough, but the process of grace has not begun.

You take another oyster shell in your hand. Open it carefully. Anything to be seen? At first it seems there is nothing. But wait. Tucked away, hidden beneath the milky substance there IS a pearl, but it is cloaked and hidden: its beauty is not apparent at all. Carefully take it in your fingers. Scrape off the mucous and wash it a little in the water. It is magnificent! A lustrous whiteness begins to glisten and glow as the clogging disfiguring material is removed. It is stunning!

Hold it in your hand with a sense of appreciation and wonderment. Describe for yourself its shape, its makeup, its color, its surface feel. Washed in the water its true radiance shines out. It delights you and makes you smile with contentment.

You realize that YOU are held in God's hands as this pearl is secure in yours.

God cherishes, admires you! God cradles you in his hands as a precious treasure enfolded in love.

You realize afresh your dignity and beauty, your true identity as God's beloved, as was long ago established in the waters of baptism. Recall the Scriptures: "You are my beloved one; with you I am well pleased"; "See what great love the Father has lavished on us, that we should be called children of God! And that is what we are!" (1 John 3:1).

Stay with this moment and linger in the waters. Let the reality of who you are in Christ penetrate your inmost being. Your worth does not come from what other people say about you. It comes from what God says about you, and God says: "You are my beloved child, with you I am well pleased!"

Pray: "God, help me to believe the truth about myself, no matter how beautiful it may be."[4] Respond to this with

---

4. Attributed to Macrina Wiederkehr.

both your head and your heart, as you celebrate the potentiality and beauty of your soul. Rejoice in the capacity of
your soul—worthy to bear the Divine within you. As Isaac
writes:

> May we see the beauty of ourselves by means of Your
>   spiritual beauty,
> that which within mortal nature stirs immortal signs.
> (3/X:21)

When you are ready, make your way gently and slowly
to the surface. Don't get the "bends" by rising too fast. Take
your time. Grace is giving new buoyancy to your soul: you
make your gradual ascent.

Hold your treasure tightly and do not let it go. The pearl
you have found is your true dignity and beauty. The pearl
you have found also symbolizes God's pure love for you,
his accepting grace. Maybe, back on land, you will be able
to share this discovery with someone? Richard Rohr tells
us, "The most courageous thing we will ever do is to bear
humbly the mystery of our own reality."[5]

---

5. Richard Rohr, *Everything Belongs* (New York: Crossroad, 2003), 97.

7. DIVING DEEP

Unearthing Pearls and Treasures

On a certain day a pearl did I take up, my brethren;
I saw in it mysteries pertaining to the Kingdom;
Semblances and types of the Majesty;
It became a fountain, and I drank out of it mysteries of the Son.
(Ephrem, *Hymn on Faith* 1)

Ephrem, the fourth-century Syrian deacon and poet who so inspired Isaac, continues:

I put it, my brethren, upon the palm of my hand,
That I might examine it:
I went to look at it on one side,
And it proved faces on all sides.
I found out that the Son was incomprehensible,
Since He is wholly Light.

In its brightness I beheld the Bright One Who cannot be clouded,
And in its pureness a great mystery. . . .

It was so that I saw there its pure conception,
The Church, and the Son within her. . . .

I saw His helpful and overflowing graces,
And His hidden things with His revealed things . . .

And as that manna which alone filled the people,
In the place of pleasant meats,
With its pleasantnesses,

So does this pearl fill me in the place of books,
And the reading thereof,
And the explanations thereof.

And when I asked if there were yet other mysteries,
   It had no mouth for me that I might hear from,
   Neither any ears wherewith it might hear me.
O Thou thing without senses, whence I have gained
new senses!

It answered me and said,
"The daughter of the sea am I, the illimitable sea!
And from that sea whence I came up it is
That there is a mighty treasury of mysteries in my
bosom!
Search thou out the sea, but search not out the Lord of
the sea!

"I have seen the divers who came down after me, when
astonied,
So that from the midst of the sea they returned to the
dry ground;
For a few moments they sustained it not.
Who would linger and be searching on into the depths
of the Godhead?"[1]

This remarkable poem written by Saint Ephrem celebrates the ways in which we can ponder and reflect on our
times of prayer, like holding a pearl in the palm of our hand
and looking at it inquisitively. We enjoy its luster and radiance and mystery. We ask ourselves what it might represent
for us, what it might teach us. For Ephrem it speaks not only
of the purity of Christ but also of the mystery of the church.
A pearl itself is a witness to transformation, for it is formed

---

1. *St. Ephraim of Syria: The Pearl—Seven Hymns on the Faith*, ed. John
Gwynn, trans. J. B. Morris, The Saint Pachomius Orthodox Library,
<http://www.ccel.org/ccel/ephraim/pearl.i.html>.

around a bit of dirt that has entered the oyster, but it changes from grit to gem, from something worthless to something beyond price. In the same way, as Ephrem exhorts us, we can marvel and wonder at what God is doing in the hidden recesses of our soul, in the deepest parts of our being, at our very core. Isaac develops this theme:

> Let us consider as oysters the prayers upon which the intellect alights, the contemplative insights, divine knowledge, wisdom, joy in spirit. (2/XXXIV:5)

> It can also happen that from time to time a certain stillness, without any insights, can fall upon a person, and the mind is gathered in and dives within itself in ineffable stupefaction. (2/VII:2)

He longs that we seek

> the discerning stirring which is set in motion all of a sudden at wonder at our coming into being and creation by God; and the moment it is set in motion in a person, he is reduced to silence in wonder and remains filled with delight from head to toes. Anyone who has been aware of such joy-filled moments will understand. (2/XVIII:18)

Small Pearls

Ephrem's poem reminds us of the value in making a review of our contemplative prayer times, to name our pearls and ask what God is saying to us through little glimpses into his mystery. We hold the pearl in the palm of our hand, as it were, and ponder its message. Isaac tells us that we will not always stumble on large pearls—dazzling moments of revelation. But small pearls are not to be despised but to be celebrated. They might include intuitions into God's working, reassurance about something, a shifted perception, a fresh way of looking at things:

> Small pearls . . . come up . . . when we dive eagerly,
> many times over, holding the breath of thoughts of this
> world during our prayers and Offices. . . . they con-
> sist of a warm sensation coming from God's grace fall-
> ing upon us, through which we will receive forgiveness
> of our sins; a sweet and peaceful fervor, a joy and sense
> of unexpected lightness; and, occasionally, the testi-
> mony of assurance concerning our firm hope, and
> specific insights concerning God's care and compas-
> sion for us. Who has not sometime experienced these
> things in stillness, each one of them in due time?
> (2/XXXIV:8–10)

Sometimes there will be something that somehow clus-
ters together other God-given insights:

> During such acts [of prayer and devotion] all of a sud-
> den someone might sometimes discover a pearl which
> in a single prayer would encompass the number of all
> the others. Sometimes a person would be standing on
> his feet, or kneeling, his mind seized by the wonder of
> prayer. (2/XIV:24)

For Isaac, the pearl is a God-given revelation, a divine
grace, a gift and not a right or due. Angels might be involved:

> This is how you should understand me with respect
> to all the insights which occur through grace—insights
> which do not come as a result of a person's investiga-
> tion or will, but occur to human nature all of a sudden,
> at the bidding of God for a person's consolation,
> through the mediation of the holy angels who are sent
> in a continual ministry to those who are going to in-
> herit life, in accordance with the word of the blessed
> Paul. (2/XVIII:20)

Cause Your hidden power to dwell in us, so that the
senses of our souls may be strengthened, in order that
our soul may mystically strike up a song filled with
wonder. And thus we sing praise with the halleluiahs
of the Watchers on high . . . as though in heaven.
(2/X:41)

Angels are close by when the mind and heart experience
"illumined stirrings" (2/XVIII:19). Somehow angels manage
to combine activity and tasks with maintaining an uninter-
rupted sense of wonder (2/XX:7).

So what is the pearl?

A Fresh Awareness of Jesus

The primary pearl is Jesus Christ himself—a deeper appreciation of him:

Naked the wise monk will go through creation in order
to find the pearl, Jesus Christ Himself. (1/XLV:218)

Remembering Saint Paul's image of the spiritual athlete,
Isaac writes,

All these are different stages in the course run, in divine
fashion, by the intellect in the stadium of this world, each
person having his gaze fixed on his crown. The crown
of the solitary is spiritual enjoyment of Christ our Lord.
Whoever has found this, has received a pledge from this
world of those things which are to come. (2/X:40)

We seek God—for Godself. We do not come to prayer
seeking anything other than an encounter with the Divine:

God Himself is richness and His riches are for us
mercy, love and goodness. (3/VI:40)

> [we believe in] The Divine Nature which is hidden
> from all—by the mysteries that You reveal to them in
> Your love. (3/VII:5)

> I am convinced . . . that is not possible to find You
> anywhere, O eternal God. . . . but only from the foun-
> tain of Your love. From this fountain . . . You pour
> forth the treasure of Your mercy, granting them [the
> seekers] revelations, as much as possible, for the sake
> of knowledge. (3/VII:6)

> You have opened Your entire treasury in our genera-
> tion and we have gained access to it. . . .You have
> made known to us in Christ hidden aspects of Your
> eternal wisdom. (3/VII:12, 18)

A Renewed Sense of Our Own Identity in Christ

But in the process of discovering God, we discover ourselves. We waken to a fresh appreciation of our beauty and
dignity, our facility to welcome the Divine, in whose image
and likeness we are fashioned:

> Grant us to see our being made new . . . .
> May we see the beauty of ourselves
> by means of Your spiritual beauty,
> that which within mortal nature
> stirs immortal signs. (3/X:22)

> I have soiled the beauty of baptism and I am sullied,
> but in You I receive a more excellent beauty. (3/VII:35)

Isaac is full of delight and praise as he realizes the extent
of human potentiality, created out of divine love. His theological anthropology—his view of humanity—rejoices in
deep truths that we should live by and remind ourselves of
frequently:

You are the Temple of God, a veritable dwelling place for the Divine: "We become holy temples by prayer, to receive within ourselves the adorable action of the Spirit." (3/VIII:14, see also 2/V:6)

You can be overshadowed by the Shekinah glory of God. (3/VIII:8, 9)

You have an altar in the heart. (3/VIII:5)

You are a priest, anointed by the Spirit, wearing the breastplate: "place on your heart the contemplation of the mysteries of our Savior, for by this God will be revealed to you in wondrous revelations." (2/XLI:2)

You have an amazing potential for God, a faculty for union with God: "The world has become mingled with God, and creation and Creator have become one!" (2/V:18)

You are begun, continued and ended in divine love! "In love did He bring the world into existence; in love does He guide it during this temporal existence; in love is He going to bring it to that wondrous transformed state." (2/XXXVIII:2)

You have a capacity for the Divine: "Praise to Your grace, O God, who brought us into existence when we did not exist, granted us an unending being, providing us with life, sense perception, reason, freewill and authority, five incomparably great gifts." (2/XVIII:18)

You are destined for eternity! "And because it was not possible that we should be like You without beginning, You granted that we should be without end, like You." (2/XVIII:18)

"To what a state is our common nature invited!"
(2/XXXVIII:1)

"He pours over us His immense grace that, like the
ocean, knows no limit." (2/XL:13)

Our value and worth does not come from what other
people think about us. Our dignity and potential come from
what God thinks about us—and it brings him joy! Isaac
prays that he may live out his baptismal identity and
vocation:

> Stir up within me the vision of Your Mysteries so that
> I may become aware of what was placed in me at holy
> baptism . . . . You have made me to be light and salt
> for the world. (2/V:14)

We join Isaac in praise for the wonder of our being:

> I give praise to Your holy Nature, Lord, for You have
> made my nature a sanctuary for Your hiddenness and
> a tabernacle for Your Mysteries, a place where You can
> dwell, and a holy temple for Your divinity. (2/V:6)

Wonderment

As we contemplate such pearls we are filled with amazement and awe:

> And often the soul in its thoughts during ecstasy will
> desist from the use of the wonted deliberations—
> natural practice—by reason of the novel experiences
> which reach it from the sea of their mysteries. Even
> when the mind is floating on its upper waters, without
> being able to make its impulses deep as the depth of
> the waters (so that it can see all the treasures in its
> abysses)—still meditation, by its power of love, will

have sufficient force to bind the thoughts firmly together with thoughts of ecstasy so that they are
checked from thinking of and running after the nature
of the body. (1/I:3)

Isaac testifies to spectacular, mesmerizing insights that
leave one speechless:

we call "truth" the right reflection on God which stems
from Him, upon which someone stumbles in their
mind, in a kind of state of wonder: *amazing thoughts
occur in the soul* at the spiritual stirrings concerning
hidden matters—a wonder at spiritual mysteries.
(2/VIII:1)

Glimpses of heaven lead to such wonderment: "by gazing
at such things the mind is changed into a state of wonder
. . . he gradually approaches the state of wonder thanks to
some awesome reflection which from time to time domi-
nates the soul" (2/VIII:14, 17).

Meanwhile, the Holy Spirit effects an overshadowing of
the soul:

the mysterious variety of overshadowing such as takes
place with any holy person, is an active force which
overshadows the intellect, and when someone is held
worthy of this overshadowing, the intellect is seized
and dilated with a sense of wonder. (2/XVI:5)

Even Isaac struggles to find words to describe this stum-
bling on pearls and divine insights:

When someone receives . . . an awareness of these
mysteries, by means of that interior eye which is called
contemplation, which consists in a mode of vision provided by grace, then the moment he becomes aware of

one of these mysteries, his heart is at once rendered serene with a kind of wonder. Not only do the lips cease from the flow of prayer and become still, but the heart too dries up from all thoughts, due to the amazement that alights upon it; and it receives from grace the sweetness of God's wisdom and love. (2/XXXV:1, 4)

Isaac's Own Pearl of Great Price

What is the greatest pearl Isaac himself uncovered? What is his greatest discovery? What is his most significant insight that he shares with us across the centuries? Without doubt, it is that at the heart of God lies unfathomable compassion and inexhaustible mercy to every one of his creatures. He delights in an awareness of "that creating and guiding power which guides creation with a care that is utterly astonishing" (2/XXXV:3). Isaac prepares us for the possibility of swimming in tears:

This will be to thee a luminous token of the serenity of thy soul: when thou, examining thyself, findest thyself full of mercy for all mankind, and when thy heart is afflicted by pity for them. . . . The body is wont to swim in tears, as the mind gazes at spiritual things, while it is as if from the eyes there flowed brooks which moisten the cheeks, without compulsion, spontaneously. (1/LXXI:330)

He goes on to celebrate this pearl of great price:

What is a merciful heart? It is the heart's burning for the sake of the entire creation, for men, for birds, for animals, for demons and for every created thing; and by the recollection and sight of them the eyes of a merciful man pour forth abundant tears. From the strong and vehement mercy which grips his heart and from his great compassion, his heart is humbled and he cannot bear to hear or see any injury or slight sorrow in creation. For this reason he continually offers up tearful prayer, even for irrational beasts, for the enemies of the truth and for those who harm him, that they be protected and receive mercy. And in like manner he even prays for the family of reptiles because of the great compassion that burns in his heart without measure in the likeness of God. (1/LXXIV:341)

All-embracing Love: Every Creature Is Precious in God's Sight

Isaac encourages us to leave behind small ideas of God. He notices that we project onto God our own human ideas of justice, vengeance, and retribution, but these are an insult to God and reveal tiny-mindedness. We should not limit God to our own narrow categories or squeeze him into a mold of our own making. Isaac is quite clear that we should quit infantile ideas about God (2/XXXIX:14). In the course of his meditative prayer, he discovers an overwhelming sense of God's mercy and how much he cherishes each individual. We are precious, and he does not inflict punishment on us. This insight shapes his whole approach to the question of "Gehenna"—hell. Such a state after death must, Isaac understands, be a temporary place marked by repentance, healing, purgation. Why would God create people only to have them condemned forever? God's foreknowledge of human proclivities must exclude the imposition of eternal punishment, which, says Isaac, is totally incompatible with the God of love. He is principally loving Father, not exacting Judge.

This understanding speaks powerfully to our contemporary world, which is often marked by the demonization of the other, a judgmentalism that is quick to condemn others, a poison of our own age that fosters prejudice and polarization. There is no favoritism or partiality within God: His

love, which is eternal, accepts all and longs for the fulfill-
ment of all:[2]

> Everyone has a single place in His purpose in the rank-
> ing of love, corresponding to the form He beheld in them
> before He created them. . . . He has a single ranking of
> complete and impassible love towards everyone, and
> He has a single caring concern for those who have fallen,
> just as much as for those who have not fallen. (2/XL:3)

"In every epoch," Alfeyev writes, "the Christian world
needs to be reminded of this universal love of God for his
creation because in every epoch there is a strong tendency
within Christianity to replace the religion of love and freedom taught by Jesus with a religion of slavery and fear."[3]

Isaac has stumbled on a great discovery and an insight
that will shape his entire writing and ministry, and he shares
it with daring and confidence:

> Among all His actions there is none which is not en-
> tirely a matter of mercy, love and compassion: this
> constitutes the beginning and the end of His dealings
> with us. . . . How much to be worshipped is our Lord
> God's gentle compassion and His immeasurable mu-
> nificence. (2/XXXIX:22)

Isaac becomes captivated by a sense of sheer amazement:

> Let us consider then, how rich in its wealth is the ocean
> of His creative act, and how many created things be-
> long to God, and how in His compassion He carries

2. Possible influences on Isaac's *Apocatastasis* or universalism are dis-
cussed in Hilarion Alfeyev, ed., *St Isaac the Syrian and His Spiritual Legacy*
(New York: St Vladimir's Seminary Press, 2015), 123ff.

3. Alfeyev, *Legacy*, 300–301.

everything, acting providentially as He guides creation; and how with a love that cannot be measured He
arrived at the establishment of the world and the beginning of creation; and how compassionate God is,
and how patient; and how He loves creation, and how
He carries it, gently enduring its importunity, the
various sins and wickedness, the terrible blasphemies
of demons and evil men. Then, once someone has
stood amazed, and filled his intellect with the majesty
of God, amazed at all these things He has done and is
doing, then he wonders in astonishment at His mercifulness, how, after all these things, God has prepared
for them another world that has no end. (2/X:19)

Isaac's conviction that the kingdom of God triumphs over
Gehenna and his sense of God's compassion emerge from
his profound mystical experience. He is offering us a paradigm shift and a fresh vison of God's grace. This is subversive
wisdom that calls into question traditional views of divine
retribution. Isaac is pushing the boundaries of our understanding of God's care for humanity and of God's commitment to humanity. His teaching springs from the deep place
of prayer, from the embrace of God that he has himself experienced in solitude and stillness. His encounter with God
becomes transformative—shattering inherited ideas about
God and opening up new vistas of grace. In a sentence:

There exists with God a single love and compassion
which is spread out over all creation, a love which is
without alteration, timeless and everlasting. (2/XL:1)

This is, indeed, Isaac's pearl of great price.[4]

---

4. We recall later spiritual writers who stumble on such a pearl. It is
expressed in the fourteenth-century *Revelations of Divine Love* by Julian
of Norwich: see Robert Llewelyn, *With Pity Not With Blame* (London:

Questions for Reflection

1. What is the greatest discovery in your spiritual life that you have made so far?

2. What insights from prayer have startled or surprised you? About God? About yourself?

3. What changes in perception and understanding have you experienced during the course of meditation or contemplation?

4. In what ways have you experienced a paradigm shift—a completely fresh way of looking at things?

5. What do you treasure as your most precious piece of spiritual knowledge?

6. Is there a way in which you can share this with others? Have you done so yet? What is stopping you?

Prayer Exercise

Reread the poem by Ephrem that prefaces this chapter. Compose a prayer or poem on a pearl of grace or insight that you have personally discovered. Be bold and imaginative in the metaphors or imagery you use to describe your discovery. Then share your poem with a spiritual director or fellow-companion on the journey.

Darton, Longman & Todd, 1989). We see it also in the great hymn by Frederick W. Faber (1854), "There's a wideness in God's mercy like the wideness of the sea," which contains the lines:

For the love of God is broader Than the measure of our mind;
And the heart of the Eternal Is most wonderfully kind . . .
But we make His love too narrow By false limits of our own;
And we magnify His strictness With a zeal He will not own.

8. HOMECOMING

May God grant you to know the power of the world to come. (2/XIII:2)

For most of us the term "The New World" conjures up images of intrepid explorers setting across the Atlantic Ocean on a quest for lands thought to be undiscovered. It derives from a letter written in 1503 by Florentine voyager Amerigo Vespucci, who offered the theory that the lands found by European explorers in the West were not the edges of Asia, as Christopher Columbus believed, but in fact an entirely different continent, a "new world." He wrote to his patrons, "In passed days I wrote very fully to you of my return from the new countries, which have been found and explored with the ships, at the cost, and by the command of this Most Serene King of Portugal; and it is lawful to call it a new world, because none of these countries were known to our ancestors, and to all who hear about them they will be entirely new."[1] The "new world" came to represent something worth sacrifice and struggle to reach, because it promised untold riches.

But in the seventh century Isaac has something very different in mind. He loves this phrase, which seems to derive

---

1. Clements Robert Markham, ed., *The Letters of Amerigo Vespucci and Other Documents Illustrative of His Career* (London: Hakluyt Society, 1894), 42.

from the Odes of Solomon: "but they shall possess incor-
ruption in the new world" (Odes 33:12). For Isaac the phrase
denotes the Life of the Age to Come, Paradise regained, the
kingdom of heaven, the New Age, the beatific vision. It
symbolizes union with the Divine.

For Isaac it is not a distant horizon, a faraway dream, but
a reality that can be enjoyed even now, here below. When
we reach the deepest places of prayer we taste heaven. As
we have noted, Isaac sketches a journey for three levels of
prayer: bodily / embodied prayer, the soul's pure prayer
of meditation and stirrings, and the Beyond—the spirit's
wordless prayer of deep silence. It is here that we can enjoy
a foretaste of the New World. When we reach the third level
of spiritual progress—moving beyond words or images or
stirrings or reflections, resting in God in deepest stillness—
then we anticipate the New World:

> In the New World none of these things [humility, la-
> bors, almsgiving . . . the mouth's sacrifices and
> prayers] is required: the spiritual mode of life consists
> in a different kind of knowledge. (2/XX:6)

We have crossed a boundary (1/XXII:112) and stumbled
into heaven, on earth! As he puts it, "Whoever has entered
the thick darkness of the knowledge of faith and has known
the power of its mysteries, is always in heaven in his intellect, and sits with Christ" (3/XI:31).

Isaac rejoices in God's providence and unfolding plan,
from time into eternity, from this world to the next:

> In love did He bring the world into existence; in love
> does He guide it during this its temporal existence; in
> love is He going to bring it to that wondrous trans-
> formed state, and in love will the world be swallowed
> up in the great mystery of Him who has performed all
> these things . . . since in the New World the Creator's
> love rules over all rational nature, the wonder at His

mysteries that will be revealed then will captivate to itself the intellect of all rational beings whom He has created so that they might have delight in Him, whether they be evil or whether they be just. (2/XXXVIII:2)

Isaac sees such reflection on the future world not as some kind of escapism or eschatological dreaming but rather as a key to inner renewal. Contemplation of our future hopes is life-giving:

The beginning of the renewal of the inner person consists, then, in the meditation and constant reflection on things to come. By this means a person is little by little purified of customary distraction on earthly things: he becomes like a snake which has sloughed off its old skin, and is renewed and rejuvenated. Similarly, inasmuch as bodily thoughts, and concern for these, diminish in the mind, accordingly reflection on things heavenly, and the gazing on things to come, increasingly springs up in the soul. (2/VIII:16)

Isaac tells us that we should always be ready for the advent of the New World—the inbreaking of the World to Come. Quoting Ephrem, he says, "we should make our soul like a ready ship that knows not when a wind will come upon it . . . if merchants are so well prepared for the sake of a little gain, though they will perhaps soon return from their voyage, how much more should we make ourselves ready, and prepare ourselves in advance, before the coming of that decisive day, that bridge and door into the new age?" (1/62:301, trans. Miller).

Journeying Now into the Future

Isaac holds in tension our reflections on a future world and our appropriation of its blessings in the here and now. He

has a keen sense that we are voyagers and travelers on a
spiritual journey or migration:

> Concern increases for the new world and care of future
> things, earnest meditation on these things and con-
> tinual migration, which is the journey of the mind to
> these things. (3/I:8)

> You are made worthy of ineffable communion with
> God the Father, which happens by means of a revela-
> tion in the journey of those who live the migration of
> the mind, as the fathers say. (3/VI:51)

In a key passage, Isaac likens the Christian to a seafarer
who ventures from island to island:

> The mind that has found spiritual wisdom is like a
> man that has found on the ocean an equipped ship
> which, when he has got aboard, brings him from the
> ocean of this world to the island of the world to be.
> Just so the apperception of the future things in this
> world, is like a small island in the ocean. And he that
> has approached unto it, he will no more be vexed by
> the storms of temporal phantasies. (1/XLV:218)

Isaac suggests that we may find temporary havens here
below, where we can experience a proleptic taste of heaven.
But our deepest longing is for the ultimate harbor of rest.
Isaac echoes the sentiment of Paul: "our homeland is in
heaven, where our Savior, the Lord Jesus Christ, is" (Phil
3:20, *The Living Bible*). We are not residents or citizens on
earth but pilgrims, just passing through: "forgetting what
lies behind and straining forward to what lies ahead, I press
on towards the goal for the prize of the heavenly call of God
in Christ Jesus" (Phil 3:13, 14). This earthly life is characterized by an insatiable search and quest and longing for

knowledge of the Divine. Isaac wants to spur us on, to keep moving and keep searching, while remaining aware of our eternal destiny. Here below we may enjoy havens of contemplative rest:

> In the early morning, when sailors
> begin to work in the world,
> in Your harbor, my Lord, our souls
> are at rest from all stirrings. (3/X:10)

> Hold Your holy ones worthy while they are still in the body of the harbor of rest. (2/V:26)

These stopping-off points, these times of stillness in the turbulent voyage, keep us going and sustain our hope and determination:

> it can also happen that from time to time a certain stillness, without any insights, can fall upon a person, and the mind is gathered in and dives within itself in ineffable stupefaction; this is the harbor full of rest of which the Fathers speak in their writings, describing how on occasion human nature enters there, when it has drawn close to the entrance point of a spiritual mode of existence . . . . It is with his eyes set on this harbor that the solitary . . . undertakes all the labor of body and soul, allowing himself to be buffeted about by all the vicissitudes which these involve. Once the solitary has come near this entrance point, henceforth he will make straight for the harbor as he draws close to the spiritual mode of being; and from this point onwards astonishing things take place for him and he receives the pledge of the New World. (2/VII:2)

Isaac asks: "After such insights [received in the prayer of wonderment], who will not laud you, O stillness, that harbor of mercies?" (2/XVIII:19).

The fears we noted in chapter two regarding "the rudder of fear" are now dissipated:

> [when] raised up to the mode of life in the spirit, to the fullest measure attainable here by human nature—immediately a state of wonder at God attaches itself to him . . . his entire mind vibrates with spiritual stirrings, accompanied by love. In this state of understanding, fear is removed from a person, and after the manner of that New World, the mind is stirred with freedom from thoughts concerning any fear or suffering . . . he is in a state of joy at God in the stirring of his thoughts at all times. (2/XX:10, 11)

Receiving Revelations of the New World in Our Prayer

Isaac rejoices: "for You came and renewed me with an awareness of the New World" (2/V:5). In the deepest places of our prayer, marked by stillness and silence, we can actually experience the peace and felicity of the New Age—what he calls "continuous exultation in the love and joy that exists in God" (2/VIII:11). We can receive glimpses of heaven. Isaac's prayer for us is, "may God grant you to know the power of the world to come" (2/XIII:2; see Heb 6:5). He affirms of prayer, "In this a mirror of the new world is received, making us taste by means of the Spirit that life beyond, which we shall receive" (3/IX:31).

He delights in the foretastes given. A key word is *revelation*: insights and perceptions received in the course of receptive prayer:

> Wonder at the divine Nature is a revelation of the New World. (2/VIII:4)

> Revelations of the New World are wondrous stirrings concerning God. With these mysteries all rational na-

ture will be stirred in that future existence, in that heavenly abode. (2/VIII:5)

> Revelations about the New World . . . concern the wondrous transformations which creation will experience, and concern each aspect of the future state as it is made known to the intellect through the revelation of various insights which are the result of continual reflection on them and illumination. (2/VIII:7)

> Revelation concerning the New World stirs up awareness. (2/XLI:2)

> This is one mysterious kind of overshadowing [by the Holy Spirit in prayer]: when this power overshadows a person, he is held worthy of the glory of the New World by means of revelation. (2/XVI:6)

The spiritual mode of life we can live here below anticipates the life of the resurrection, when we are with the holy angels. The disciplined life of the monk—called in monastic tradition "the angelic life"—marked as it is by wonderment, silence, and a release from physical concerns—becomes an image of the life to come: "the ascetic conduct of the inner person is a symbol of existence after the resurrection: this does not make use of bodily actions, but is brought about and received by the stirrings of the mind. . . . Yonder [are] delightful gaze and vison without distraction" (2/VIII:2). Isaac sees the monk as modeling a different type of life that bespeaks eternity, a way of living that reveals the Divine in the midst of the earthly, a kind of icon that points to another set of values and to a wider vision.[2]

---

2. See Patrik Hagman, *The Asceticism of Isaac of Nineveh* (Oxford: Oxford University Press, 2010); Jason Scully, *Isaac of Nineveh's Ascetical Eschatology* (Oxford: Oxford University Press, 2018).

We can begin now, as it were, to practice and rehearse something of the life to come, marked by freedom: "Undo from my outer senses the manifest restraints, so I may run to enter the Paradise of Your mysteries and eat of the Tree of Life from which Adam was not allowed to eat" (2/V:20). Liberty blends with joy as we discover even now the freedom of the children of God (see Rom 8:21). In a delightful phrase, Isaac tells us that we can inhale the oxygen of heaven here below: "Thus he smells life from God, that lives with love in this creation. He breathes here of the air of resurrection. In this air the righteous will delight at resurrection" (1/XLIII:211). Conversely, Isaac warns us that we can't breathe the clear fresh air of the new world if we immerse ourselves in the earthly cares of this world (1/LXXIX:362).

Further Voyages Now Beckon Us

In this book we have seen how Isaac encourages us to see the spiritual life as a voyage of discovery, and to view the practice of prayer as an adventure in which we may make astonishing explorations. Isaac longs both to affirm his readers in their spiritual practice and also to stretch them, to urge them ever deeper into the ocean of God's grace, where so many treasures are waiting to be discovered. While sharing great wisdom that comes from his firsthand experience, he is not prescriptive: there is a diversity of paths and routes through the ocean:

> This meditation and converse directed towards God has many paths, each person taking the path for which his understanding is capable and on which he can make progress, drawing closer to God on it as a result of daily experience. . . . there are many paths for this converse which exists with God in stillness, and everyone, insofar as he approaches His presence with

understanding, will accordingly choose the path suitable to his measure. Not that every path will prove
successful for everyone, but for everyone, in that he
shares in the interior upbringing of the way of life,
conscience will indicate which path to take . . .
through the grace which stirs up in him testimony
from within; it will instruct him by indicating its hidden path. (2/XXX:2, 3)

The important thing is to keep moving:

Do you then, O fellow human being, choose one of
these paths that suits your measure and your understanding. Travel along it . . . . Show your entire aim
to be directed towards God alone, and travel on the
path that leads to Him. As far as you are able, be in
continual recollection of Him, and the path will go
easily and without a break, as you beseech Him con-
tinuously. (2/XXX:13)

Realize, says Isaac, that we have not arrived: God is ever
summoning us deeper. He is yearning that we keep developing our skills of spiritual swimming. We need a holy
restlessness and a refusal to think that we have understood
it all. In fact, we have only dipped our toe in the water, as
it were—God's ocean of grace is boundless, without boundaries or limits, unfathomable. It calls us daily: it invites us
to take the plunge and move beyond our present experience.
We have only just begun:

And just as our rational nature has already become
gradually more illumined and wise in a holy understanding of the mysteries which are hidden in Scripture's discourse about God . . . so too we shall in the
future come to know and be aware of many things for
which our present understanding will be seen as

contrary to what it will be then; and the whole order-
ing of things yonder will undo any precise opinion we
possess now in our supposition about Truth. For there
are many, indeed endless, things which do not even
enter our minds here. (2/XXXIX:19)

In prayer we are summoned to ever-expanding horizons,
ever more stunning treasures. If we remain utterly open
and determined in the spiritual quest, we will come to see
things differently, we will revise our inherited concepts yet
again. We dare not predict what we will find out. God summons us to unfolding revelation, an adventure without
limit, ever more discoveries to make. The depths ever summon us afresh.

Toward the end of Part 3 Isaac sums up his teaching with
affirmations and with an encouragement for his readers that
resounds across the centuries and finds an echo in our own
soul today:

Therefore, from when the mind begins to be enlight-
ened, after it has settled and rested a little from the
battle, the tumult of the passions, and the distraction
of empty intentions which disturb its vision—this
wonder of thoughts begins to appear upon it, by means
of the intelligible light of the mind.

Many times a day, wonderful stirrings arise in it,
and the mind is gathered within itself and stays tran-
quil and the person sits silent and astonished. This
occurs sometimes at moments of prayer or sometimes
at the Office. How pleasant, then, is this silence and
this calm! Who knows this, except those who have
been overshadowed! . . .

There is possibility of delay in this, according to the
measure of the mind. The mind, then, does not reach
these realities whenever it wishes, or as often as it
asks. . . . This gathering together of the mind and the

vision of the intellect is the fruit of great separation from others, from prudence concerning thoughts and the fight against passions. And as I said, every time that this gathering together of the mind and the marvelous stirring occurs, at the beginning there is a brief moment; then the mind returns to what is its own, until other stirrings happen again.

So when the solitary has arrived at this order, and this sweetness is mingled with his hidden work with God, then he is uplifted a little from listlessness. His soul is not afflicted by the stillness or the long separation from others, nor by the afflictions or the infirmities of the body, as at one time. In that the delight of his mind and the consolation of his heart remove these adversities far from him . . . .

But when by this he is a little refreshed, then the difficult way of the solitary life becomes easy in his eyes. Now this which I have already said, I repeat, as a reminder for those who long for these realities: that these delights and apperceptions happen when grace rests upon the mind and it takes on the power of the Spirit . . . .

May the Lord grant you this, that it will not only be from simple reading that you know these things, but that in the experience of your person you may know, feel and taste these things, by means of the grace of the holy Spirit which rests upon your intellect. Amen. (3/XV:18–24)

Questions for Reflection

1. Have you experienced foretastes of heaven in your prayer? Can you describe them?

2. What difference do you think it would make to place your current practice of prayer within a cosmic context, a perspective spanning heaven and earth, as Isaac's thought reveals?

3. How far have you traveled in the course of this book? What discoveries have you made?

4. To what fresh expressions or practices of prayer do you sense God is now summoning you?

5. What is your next step on the spiritual journey?

Prayer Exercise

Take time to review your own progress and the movements in your soul during the course of using this resource. Take stock: Where are you now with God? What do you now long for at this point? Do you need to name and identify any barriers or hesitations that hold you back from an adventurous journey with God? Express to God your deepest yearnings and surrender to God your resolves. Conclude by making your own the prayer of Saint Isaac:

> O Mystery . . . beyond every word and beyond silence, who became human in order to renew us by means of voluntary union with the flesh, reveal to me the path by which I may be raised up to Your mysteries, traveling along a course that is clear and tranquil, free from the illusions of this world. Gather my mind into the silence of prayer, so that wandering thoughts may be silenced within me during that illumined converse of supplication and mystery-filled wonder. (2/V:7)

And don't forget—hold on to the pearls you have discovered. Let no one rob you:

> Be alert . . . and be like a prudent merchant, bearing thy pearl and wandering through the world, anxious that its excellent beauty be not besmirched. Be careful, lest it be stolen from thee. (1/XXIV:121)

Above all, rejoice in what God gives you in prayer and be ready to hearten others in their spiritual journey:

> For the hand of the Lord which taught our Fathers about the spiritual swimming . . . and about confidence in the sea-journey so full of riches, is not too small to grant us too, in His own time, strong arms which will reach out over the waves of the fearful sea in order to reach those places from which our Fathers brought up spiritual treasures. (2/XXXIV:12)

APPENDIX 1:
BIBLICAL RESOURCES

From this reading of Scripture, limitless prayer is generated. (3/IX:12)

The most formative influence on Isaac's thought is the prayerful and meditative reading of Scripture. For him, Scripture is the seedbed of prayer. It is a springboard for diving into the depths of prayer. The reading of biblical texts, Isaac writes,

> moves the senses of the soul to look into the hidden mystery of divine wisdom. It brings one to the understanding of its incomprehensibility . . . . It makes one marvel at the hidden Essence [of God] . . . . It brings forth the riches of His love, revealed to all and ready, indeed, to be spread abroad. (3/IX:9; see also 2/XXI:13)

Here we explore the general biblical background to Isaac's playful and prayerful approach to the theme, and we remind ourselves of the way Scripture celebrates both the physicality of the sea and the spirituality of the sea. We look at the nautical imagery that the Scriptures give us—alluded to explicitly by Isaac or just in the hinterland of his thinking, immersed and saturated as it was by the waters of the divine words. We explore three major biblical themes: divine creativity, risk and adventure, the summons of Jesus.

We conclude with three biblical challenges from the deep that will launch us on our adventure. But let's begin with the great biblical theme of the search for God.

The Spiritual Quest

The biblical texts draw us again and again to the depths. They convey aching places of the human soul:

> Out of the depths I cry to you, O LORD.
> Lord, hear my voice! (Ps 130:1)

The spiritual quest is a theme running through the Scriptures and surfacing clearly in the gospels and the Pauline writings. It is in the background when Isaac teaches about developing an expectancy to discover more of God in prayer, while realizing that such pearls are not easily unearthed. The theme of searching for the Divine weaves its way through the Hebrew Scriptures:

> Seek the LORD while he may be found,
> call upon him while he is near. (Isa 55:6)

The depths speak of divine profundities. The seeker after wisdom wonders to himself where God is to be found:

> That which is, is far off, and deep, very deep; who can find it out? I turned my mind to know and to search out and to seek wisdom and the sum of things. (Eccl 7:24, 25)

The Wisdom literature is a search for meaning and insight:

> If you indeed cry out for insight,
> and raise your voice for understanding;
> if you seek it like silver,

and search for it as for hidden treasures—
then you will understand the fear of the LORD
and find the knowledge of God. (Prov 2:3-5)

More than any other part of Scripture, Isaac loves to quote the Psalms. Isaac encourages those reciting Psalms to allow them to trigger meditation, in which one can follow the course of one's reflections and leave the Office behind: the Psalms become the starting point for such dives into prayer. There we often encounter the theme of yearning, longing for more of God, deep desire for an encounter with the Divine:

My soul thirsts for God,
for the living God.
When shall I come and behold
the face of God?
Deep calls to deep
at the thunder of your cataracts;
all your waves and your billows
have gone over me. (Ps 42:2, 7)

The Spiritual Quest in the Gospels

After the Psalms, it is the gospels that Isaac loves to quote or allude to. Matthew's gospel gives us not only the parable of the pearl but also the parable of the hidden treasure:

The kingdom of heaven is like treasure hidden in a field, which someone found and hid; then in his joy he goes and sells all that he has and buys that field. (Matt 13:44)

These sayings are not found in the other gospels. They reflect the theme of searching and hiddenness that is introduced in the nativity narratives with the search of the wise men, archetypal figures representing every man and every woman in their dedicated odyssey and quest for the redeemer. The theme of hiddenness is celebrated throughout chapter 13, where Matthew gathers together the parables of the kingdom of heaven. Matthew writes about "the secrets of the Kingdom of Heaven" (13:11). Jesus here quotes the psalmist's words: "I will open my mouth to speak in parables; I will proclaim what has been hidden from the foundation of the world" (Matt 13:35; see Ps 78:2). All vital things seem to be hidden:

> the seed, to be fruitful, must be planted deep in the
>   earth (Matt 13:23),
> the grain of mustard seed is likewise placed into the soil,
> the yeast is deliberately concealed: "The kingdom of
> heaven is like leaven which a woman took and hid in
> three measures of flour." (Matt 13:33, RSV)

Luke's gospel develops the theme of searching. How does Jesus respond to the request, "Lord, teach us to pray"? He invites us to become persistent searchers in prayer: "So I say to you, Ask, and it will be given you; search, and you will find . . . . For everyone who asks receives, and everyone who searches finds" (Luke 11:9, 10). Prayer is here depicted as a search, a quest. Prayer, Jesus suggests, can become curious, inquisitive.

God himself is depicted as a searcher in chapter 15. As a shepherd he seeks out the lost sheep. Like a woman he hunts for a mislaid coin. Like a father, he longs for his lost son. Luke also develops the theme of opening our eyes to glimpse divine revelation. This is clearest in the Emmaus story, which moves from "their eyes were kept from recognizing him" (Luke 24:16) on the road to, "Then their eyes were opened, and they recognized him" (Luke 24:31) at the breaking of the bread. Isaac finds himself making the prayer,

"Make me worthy to behold You with opened eyes which are more interior than the eyes of the body" (3/VII:33).

Jesus delights too in the theme of treasure:

> Do not store up for yourselves treasures on earth, where moth and rust consume and where thieves break in and steal; but store up for yourselves treasures in heaven, where neither moth nor rust consumes and where thieves do not break in and steal. For where your treasure is, there your heart will be also. (Matt 6:19-21; compare Luke 12:33-34)

The Pauline writings cherish this theme of riches:

> In him we have redemption through his blood, the forgiveness of our trespasses, according to the riches of his grace. (Eph 1:7)

> so that in the ages to come he might show the immeasurable riches of his grace in kindness toward us in Christ Jesus. (Eph 2:7)

The writer weaves together the theme of treasure with that of the mystery and revelation of Christ. The letter to the Colossians offers this prayer: "I want their hearts to be encouraged and united in love, so that they may have all the riches of assured understanding and have the knowledge of God's mystery, that is, Christ himself, in whom are hidden all the treasures of wisdom and knowledge" (Col 2:2-3).

The writer of Colossians marvels at "the mystery that has been hidden throughout the ages and generations but has now been revealed to his saints" (Col 1:26). He speaks of "the riches of the glory of this mystery, which is Christ in you, the hope of glory" (Col 1:27). He prays that his readers will gain "the riches of assured understanding and have the knowledge of God's mystery, that is, Christ himself" (Col 2:2). But while we are invited to revelation, paradoxically we are being called to hiddenness, where "your life is hidden with Christ in God" (Col 3:3).

Mystery becomes a key word in Ephesians:

> he has made known to us the mystery of his will, according to his good pleasure that he set forth in Christ (Eph 1:9)

> the mystery was made known to me by revelation (Eph 3:3)

> perceive my understanding of the mystery of Christ (Eph 3:4)

> In former generations this mystery was not made known to humankind, as it has now been revealed to his holy apostles and prophets by the Spirit. (Eph 3:5)

The Holy Spirit Brings Us Revelations of the Divine

For Paul, it is the Holy Spirit who leads us into the depths:

> These things God has revealed to us through the Spirit; for the Spirit searches everything, even the depths of God. (1 Cor 2:10)

> Likewise the Spirit helps us in our weakness; for we do not know how to pray as we ought, but that very Spirit intercedes with sighs too deep for words. (Rom 8:26)

Above all, the image of the depths summons us to plumb the unfathomable love of God:

> I pray that, according to the riches of his glory, he may grant that you may be strengthened in your inner being with power through his Spirit, and that Christ may dwell

in your hearts through faith, as you are being rooted and
grounded in love. I pray that you may have the power
to comprehend, with all the saints, what is the breadth
and length and height and depth, and to know the love
of Christ that surpasses knowledge, so that you may be
filled with all the fullness of God. (Eph 3:16-18)

Isaac delights in this passage and refers to it several times:[1]

But we speak God's wisdom, secret and hidden, which
God decreed before the ages for our glory . . . as it is
written, "What no eye has seen, nor ear heard,
nor the human heart conceived,
what God has prepared for those who love him";
these things God has revealed to us through the Spirit;
for the Spirit searches everything, even the depths of
God. (1 Cor 2:7-10)

For Paul, the Holy Spirit works at a very deep level: as
Charles K. Barrett puts it "The Spirit thus enables inward
apprehension of profound divine truth."[2] James Kinn observes, "Paul's point is that the Spirit alone is capable of
revealing the mystery of God, since only the Spirit has in-
timate knowledge of God."[3] Isaac echoes this conviction.

The Beckoning Sea
Divine Creativity

The earth was without form and void, and darkness
was upon the face of the deep; and the Spirit of God
was moving over the face of the waters. (Gen 1:2, RSV)

1. 1/II:8; 2/XXIV:2; 3/IX:20, 31; 3/III:36; 3/V:4.
2. Charles K. Barrett, *A Commentary on the First Epistle to the Corinthians*
(London: A & C Black, 1968), 75.
3. James W. Kinn, *The Spirit of Jesus in Scripture and Prayer* (Lanham,
MD: Sheed & Ward, 2004), 14.

The Bible opens with a picture of the Spirit of God, the divine breath hovering over the surface of the primordial ocean: a mighty wind sweeping over dark waters, poised to bring order and meaning to a universe of chaos:

> At first the earth lacked shape and was totally empty, and a dark fog draped over the deep while God's spirit-wind hovered over the surface of the empty waters. Then there was the voice of God. (Gen 1:2, *The Voice*)

The very creation itself begins in the waters of the deep. As Isaac reflected on the significance of the ocean lapping the shores of his native land, his mind went back to such Scriptures, which shape our imagination and our understanding of God's creative ways:

> The One who made the Pleiades and Orion,
> and turns deep darkness into the morning,
> and darkens the day into night,
> who calls for the waters of the sea,
> and pours them out on the surface of the earth,
> the LORD is his name. (Amos 5:8)

The Wisdom literature, and especially the Book of Job, marvels at the mystery of God as it contemplates the waters of the deep:

> Can you find out the deep things of God?
> Can you find out the limit of the Almighty? . . .
> Its measure is longer than the earth,
> and broader than the sea. (Job 11:7, 9)

The book of Job culminates with God's questions:

> Who shut in the sea with doors
> when it burst out from the womb? . . .

> Have you entered into the springs of the sea,
> or walked in the recesses of the deep? (Job 38:8, 16)

The Psalms celebrate the power of God discerned in wind and wave:

> More majestic than the thunders of mighty waters,
> more majestic than the waves of the sea, majestic on
> high is the Lord! (Ps 93:4)

> The voice of the Lord is over the waters; the God of
> glory thunders, the Lord, over mighty waters. (Ps 29:3)

The Sea as Metaphor

Psalms begin to explore the metaphorical messages of the sea:

> You silence the roaring of the seas, the roaring of their
> waves, the tumult of the peoples. (Ps 65:7)

> God is our refuge and strength,
> a very present help in trouble.
> Therefore we will not fear, though the earth should
> change,
> though the mountains shake in the heart of the sea;
> though its waters roar and foam,
> though the mountains tremble with its tumult. . . .
> "Be still, and know that I am God!" (Ps 46:1-3, 10)

The prophet Isaiah too utilizes the tumult of the sea as a symbol of humanity's consternation:

> They will roar over it on that day,
> like the roaring of the sea. (Isa 5:30)

> But the wicked are like the tossing sea
> that cannot keep still;
> its waters toss up mire and mud. (Isa 57:20)

But paradoxically, the same sea can speak positively and become an image of God's unbounded and unlimited care:

> If I take the wings of the morning
> and settle at the farthest limits of the sea,
> even there your hand shall lead me,
> and your right hand shall hold me fast. (Ps 139:9, 10)

The prophet Habakkuk also glimpses the vastness of hope that rises in his soul as he contemplates the oceans:

> The earth will be filled
> with the knowledge of the glory of the LORD,
> as the waters cover the sea. (Hab 2:14)

Risk and Adventure

In the Ancient Near East the sea had always been viewed as a place of danger. As far back as the Babylonian *Epic of Gilgamesh*, the deep witnessed the scene of ferocious struggle between divinity and demons, while the Ugarit texts speak of Baal fighting with the sea-god Yam. In the Old Testament, God as king of creation wrestles with the dark powers of the ocean, the sea dragons of Leviathan and Rahab. This conflict looks back to the primeval chaos before creation (Gen 1:1) and looks forward to the end-time victory over the sea beast (Dan 7). Isaiah looks forward to this defeat of negativity:

> In that day the LORD will punish Leviathan the fleeing
> serpent, With His fierce and great and mighty sword,
> Even Leviathan the twisted serpent; And He will kill
> the dragon who lives in the sea. (Isa 27:1, NASB)

Job marvels at the power of God, "who alone stretched out the heavens and trampled the back of the sea dragon" (Job 9:8). The psalm declares, "You divided the sea by your might; you broke the heads of the dragons in the waters" (Ps 74:13). This worldview is picked up when Jesus stills the storm. His command to the elements is normally translated "Peace! Be still!" but the Greek is literally "Be muzzled!" (Mark 5:39)—the same words with which he expels the demon in the synagogue (Mark 1:25). Jesus speaks to the demons and dragons of the deep, echoing the longing of the psalmist: "Praise the Lord from the earth, you sea monsters and all deeps" (Ps 148:7).

Psalm 107:24-27 gives us a sense of the awesome dangers on the sea:

> Some went down to the sea in ships,
> Doing business on the mighty waters;
> They saw the deeds of the Lord,
> His wondrous works in the deep.
> For he commanded and raised the stormy wind,
> Which lifted up the waves of the sea.
> They mounted up to heaven, they went down to the depths;
> Their courage melted away in their calamity;
> They reeled and staggered like drunkards,
> And were at their wits' end.

Jonah experienced these events for himself:

> You cast me into the deep,
> into the heart of the seas,
> And the flood surrounded me;
> all your waves and your billows passed over me.
> (Jonah 2:3)

For Jonah, the sea becomes the place where he discovers the presence of God in a totally unexpected way: the place of danger becomes the place of salvation. Formerly, he had thought that God's presence was localized and limited to the temple in Jerusalem, and that in fleeing the Holy Land he was escaping the mission God had called him to do. But in the waves he discovers both God's persistent presence and God's persistent call. God says in the prophet Isaiah, "I have called you by name, you are mine. When you pass through the waters, I will be with you" (Isa 43:1b, 2a). Vocation and risk seem to be very closely linked.

Jesus' Triple Imperatives
"Follow me!"

> As he walked by the Sea of Galilee, he saw two brothers, Simon, who is called Peter, and Andrew his brother, casting a net into the sea—for they were fishermen. And he said to them, "Follow me." (Matt 4:18)

Jesus uttered his summons to the first disciples as he walked along the shoreline of the Sea of Galilee, the choppy waters lapping at his feet and stretching out before him. The shore represented safety and security, but maybe Jesus was pointing across the waters when he spoke his invitation to discipleship? Dare we move out of our comfort zone, represented by feet firmly planted on *terra firma*, and venture forth to do things differently? Dare we, as it were, leave behind the security of being on land and move out into uncharted waters? The shoreline represents the limit of our own confidence, the edge of our sense of security, but it also suggests the brink of new possibilities. This is a threshold we must cross if we are to live as pilgrims in this world, people on the move, people going places with God. At one point we read, "He told his disciples to have a boat ready for him" (Mark 3:9). Jesus has challenging journeys in store for his disciples.

"Launch into the Deep!"

This first challenge resonates with the summons Jesus gave to Peter at the Sea of Galilee: "Put out into the deep!" (Luke 5:4). The sea invites us to quit the unproductive shallows (where no fish were found all night). Fruitfulness in discipleship and a richer harvest are to be found out in the deep. The shallows represent the unadventurous Christian life, where we are content to paddle. But Jesus summons Peter, and us too, to a riskier adventure of faith.

"Cross Over to the Other Side!"

Jesus beckons his disciples across the lake. Many times in the gospels Jesus says, "Let us go over to the other side." He asks his disciples to quit the security of Capernaum, a conservative, traditional, mainly Jewish town, where Peter has a living and a house. Jesus points across the waters and challenges his disciples to traverse the lake to go to enemy territory, pagan, heathen Gentile terrain, Greco-Roman land (the Decapolis), shores where unclean demoniacs and Gadarene pigs lurk uncontrolled (Mark 5:1-20). This is a challenge to enter a different world, to encounter another worldview, to begin to see things differently.

Three Challenges from the Seas
Face Impossibilities

The biblical image of the sea is multifaceted. The seas of terror and primordial chaos can become the very locus of salvation, the place of deliverance, where God's people begin to wake up to their true identity and vocation, as the Exodus narratives remind us. The Song of Moses celebrates the victory of God:

> In the greatness of your majesty you overthrew your
> adversaries . . .
> At the blast of your nostrils the waters piled up,
> the floods stood up in a heap;
> the deeps congealed in the heart of the sea. . . .
> You blew with your wind, the sea covered them;
> they sank like lead in the mighty waters.
> Who is like you, O LORD, among the gods?
> Who is like you, majestic in holiness,
> awesome in splendor, doing wonders? (Exod 15:7-11)

The Red Sea invites us to confront our fears and anxieties about the future—represented in the uncertain waves. We are crippled into inaction by fear—sometimes we may hang back from a new venture or new expression of ministry or prayer by the fear of failure. The Sea can represent the fear of the unknown: aspects of mission that are for us yet unexplored or unfamiliar waters. The Israelites hovering on the brink of the Red Sea (or Sea of Reeds) in the exodus faced the impossibility of crossing the angry and formidable waters, and the risk of being trapped by the pursuing forces of the pharaoh.

To his surprise, the key to salvation was in Moses' own hand, and it was with his action of striking the waters that the miracle of the splitting of the sea occurred. In Jewish spirituality, the "splitting of the seas" has become a powerful symbol of facing the impossible with God: God makes the impossible possible, but needs men and women to be prepared to plunge into a risky synergy with the Divine.

In the gospel, Gabriel says to Mary, "Nothing will be impossible with God." Mary helps make the impossible happen with her words of surrender: "Here I am, the servant of the Lord; let it be with me according to your word" (Luke 1:37, 38). Seventy times in the Bible the words *Do not be afraid* occur. The parting of the waters of the sea reminds us that, with God, breakthroughs are possible.

Catch the Wind

Paul discovers the sea to be a place of risk and danger. Paul faces tempestuous winds and a life-threatening storm as his boat drifts across the thunderous sea and meets destruction on the rocks. This shipwreck seems to be the end (Acts 27:41), but in God's purposes it becomes the start of an unexpected mission, to the island of Malta. And from Malta, Paul continues by ship to Rome itself, "preaching the Kingdom of God and teaching about our Lord Jesus Christ" (Acts 28:31).

The Acts of the Apostles tells us about the wind, or breath of God, opening up new possibilities. When Luke likens the Spirit of Pentecost to a wind, he does not have in mind a gentle, soothing breeze. Rather, he writes, "And suddenly from heaven there came a sound like a rush of a violent wind . . . and all of them were filled with the Holy Spirit" (Acts 2:2, 4). We are invited to expose our lives to a Spirit who may disturb and discomfort us, as well as empowering and energizing us. It is a Spirit over which we have no control: "The wind blows where it chooses, and you hear the sound of it, but you do not know where it comes from or where it goes. So it is with everyone who is born of the Spirit" (John 3:8). As Luke's graphic account of Paul's voyage across the Mediterranean reminds us, the important thing is that we hoist the sails and catch the wind:

> When a moderate south wind began to blow, they thought they could achieve their purpose; so they weighed anchor and began to sail past Crete, close to the shore. But soon a violent wind, called the north-easter, rushed down from Crete. Since the ship was caught and could not be turned head-on into the wind, we gave way to it and were driven. (Acts 27:13-15)

Later, when they sought to land, "they cast off the anchors and left them in the sea. At the same time they

loosened the ropes that tied the steering oars; then hoisting
the foresail to the wind, they made for the beach" (Acts
27:40). Luke gives us a vivid picture of the need to stay alert
to changing wind direction and to follow the signs of the
wind's movement. Boats on the sea do not travel in a
straight line: they must continually reorient themselves in
order to catch the wind. We must take the risk of exposing
ourselves, without guard, to the Spirit of God. We look to
God for new reserves of courage: "God did not give us a
spirit of timidity, but a spirit of power, of love and self control" (2 Tim 1:7).

Become Navigators

The sea represents to us the unpredictable conditions of life
in a postmodern world, where the old and trusted landmarks
are fast disappearing. Today's church needs Christians with
pilgrim hearts, navigators who can read the unfolding signs
of the times, much like map readers who can spot the traditional reference points. Paul lists as one of the gifts of the Spirit
kubernetes; lamely translated "administration" (1 Cor 12:28,
RSV), it means "navigation" or "helmsmanship." For Paul,
the art of discerning the Spirit's movement, the art of recognizing the need of the moment, is akin to the skill of the ship's
pilot and steersman, who, working collaboratively alongside
the captain, coxswain, and entire crew, will guide the ship in
its adventures. In the seventh century John Climacus of Sinai
speaks of the need for courageous spiritual directors using
this image: "A ship with a good navigator comes safely to
port, God willing."[4] Ancient mariners looked out for the
morning star to guide and reassure them: that is a name given
to the risen Christ (Rev 22:16; see 2 Pet 1:19). Likewise, Isaac

---

4. *John Climacus: The Ladder of Divine Ascent*, trans. Colm Luibheid (New
York: Paulist Press, 1982), 259.

speaks of the need for navigation and reference points in the spiritual journey.

At about the same time as Isaac was writing, the image of navigation was central to the experience of the Celtic Christians, who had lively traditions of peregrination and voyaging on the rough seas around Ireland and Scotland. They were motivated by a desire both to spread the Gospel and to discover God's providence in the deep. The sixth-century *Voyage of Brendan* tells us,

> St Brendan then embarked, and they set sail. . . . They had a fair wind, and therefore no labour, only to keep the sails properly set; but after twelve days the wind fell to a dead calm, and they had to labour at the oars until their strength was nearly exhausted. Then St Brendan would encourage and exhort them: "Fear not, brothers, for our God will be unto us a helper, a mariner, and a pilot; take in the oars and helm, keep the sails set, and may God do unto us, His servants and His little vessel, as He wills."[5]

The ancient liturgy of the Ethiopian Church also calls on God as pilot:

> Pilot of the soul, leader of righteousness, refuge of salvation, grant us, Lord, to have eyes trained so that we may always see you, and ears to hear only your Word . . . . Grant us a pure heart so that we may always appreciate your goodness, you kind one and lover of the world!

Let's echo that prayer!

---

5. Denis O'Donoghue, trans., *St. Brendan the Voyager in Story and Legend* (Dublin: Browne & Nolan, 1895), 120.

Questions for Reflection

1. What nautical or sea images speak to you from the Old Testament?

2. Which challenges from the Sea of Galilee strike you the most? Why?

3. What can we learn about the spiritual gift of navigating our soul (*kubernetes*) from the physical art of helmsmanship?

4. How do you feel yourself responding to the metaphor of sea and boat?

APPENDIX 2.
RETREAT RESOURCES

Note: Each participant should have a copy of this book. Reflections here are short (30-minute) addresses given by the retreat leader summarizing content from the book, directing attention to selected quotations from Isaac. In this way, the words and wisdom of Isaac enter into our midst.

Diving for Pearls: Exploring the Depths of Prayer with Isaac the Syrian
Quiet Day / Day Retreat

10	Gather, coffee
10:30	Reflection 1. Quitting the Shoreline—encountering the ocean of grace (chapter 2)
11–11:30	Silence: prayer exercise from chapter 2
11:30	Reflection 2. Embracing Transitions (chapter 6)
12–12:30	Silence: questions for reflection from chapter 6
12:30	Lunch break
1:15	Reflection 3. Introduce extended prayer exercise (chapter 6)
1:30	Silence for "diving"
2:30	Reflection alone or in pairs on the pearl discovered or sought
3	Eucharist or closing prayers
	Tea and Departure

24-Hour Retreat—Overnight
Day 1

3:30   Arrival and coffee

4   Introduction and Reflection 1. Quitting the Shoreline—encountering the ocean of grace (the three oceans and the ship of your soul) (chapter 2)

5   First prayer exercise from chapter 2—your voyage thus far

6:30   Supper

8   Reflection 2. Risking the Depths (chapter 4)

Day 2

9   Extended prayer exercise from chapter 6: Starting to Dive

10:30 Coffee

11:30 Reflection 3. Diving Deep (chapter 7)

12   Reflect on your prayer experience using questions 1–3 from chapter 7, in pairs or alone

12:30 Write a poem or prayer to bring to closing worship using the prayer exercise (chapter 7)

1   Lunch

2:30   Closing worship and departure

Two-Night Retreat
Day 1

10:30 Arrival and coffee

11   Introduction: Appendix 1. The spiritual quest

12   Silent preparation: What are you seeking? What are you longing for? What is your heart's deepest desire? What questions arise in your soul?

1	Lunch
	Free time / rest
3	Reflection 1. Quitting the Shoreline (the three oceans and the ship of your soul) (chapter 2)
3:45	Silence. First prayer exercise from chapter 2: Your voyage thus far
4:30	Break
5	Silence. Second prayer exercise from chapter 2: The ocean of your soul / your ship (responses can be sketched)
6:30	Supper
7:30	Reflection 2. Risking the Depths (chapter 4)
8:30	Prayer exercise from chapter 4

Day 2

9:30	Reflection 3. Facing the Currents (chapter 5)
10:15	Questions for reflection (chapter 5)
11	Coffee
11:30	Reflection 4. Diving Deep—the sort of pearls one might find (chapter 7)
12:15	Second prayer exercise from chapter 5: Sinking
1	Lunch
	Rest
3	Extended prayer exercise from chapter 6
5:30	Reflect on your prayer experience using questions 1–3 from chapter 7, in pairs or alone
6:30	Supper
7:30	Write a poem or prayer to bring to closing worship using prayer exercise (chapter 7)

Day 3

9:30   Reflection 5: Homecoming (chapter 8)

10:30   Silence (or in pairs): Questions 3–5 (chapter 8)

11:30   Closing worship

12   Departure

"Retreat in Daily Life"

Monday   Quitting the Shoreline

Chapter 2: Encountering the three oceans and the ship of your soul

First prayer exercise from chapter 2: Your voyage thus far

Tuesday   Facing the Currents

Chapter 5: First prayer exercise from chapter 5: What is surfacing? What rising currents can you recognize?

Wednesday   Embracing Transitions

Chapter 6: Second prayer exercise from chapter 5: Sinking

Thursday Diving

Chapter 7: Diving Deep: the sort of pearls one might find

Extended prayer exercise from chapter 6

Friday   Chapter 8: Homecoming

Silence (or in pairs): Questions 3–5 (chapter 8)

Outline for a Short Course / Lenten Course

Use the questions in each chapter to stimulate group discussion and reflection.

1. Preparing
   Appendix 1: Biblical background to the spiritual search and theme of mystery / revelation

2. Quitting the Shoreline

3. Learning to Swim
   Chapter 3: Essential attitudes and spiritual disciplines

4. Embracing Transitions
   Extended meditation: Prayer exercise from chapter 6

5. Sharing
   Chapter 7: Diving Deep—the sort of pearls we might find

Resources for Worship

Use Psalms and Scriptures cited in chapter 3 and chapter 4.

Hymns
   Charles Wesley (1707–1788) sings:
   Jesus, lover of my soul,
   let me to thy bosom fly,
   while the nearer waters roll,
   while the tempest still is high.
   Hide me, O my Savior, hide,
   till the storm of life is past;
   safe into the haven guide;
   O receive my soul at last.

   John Mason (1645–1694) celebrates God's greatness:
   How great a being, Lord, is thine. . . .
   Thy knowledge is the only line

To sound so vast a deep.
Thou art a sea without a shore.

F. W. Faber (1814–1863) developed this theme:
There's a wideness in God's mercy
like the wideness of the sea.

Planning a Quiet Day / Retreat—Checklist

Aim: Clarify what you hope will happen, what difference it will make.

Structure: Schedule timings, schedule, balance of elements, silence / input.

Theme: Consider how will this inspire, challenge, hearten, teach.

Content: How will you give input? With what methods?

Process: What is going on spiritually? What shifts or transformations do you hope for?

Variety: Allow for different prayer practices or spiritual exercises.

Materials, resources: Remember to include the team, music, worship requirements, and catering.

Place, setting: Consider whether the environment is conducive to prayer.

Promotion and evaluation: How will you get feedback?

Anything else that needs to be considered, such as disability issues and other special needs of people, etc.

Bibliography

Primary Sources
Isaac the Syrian

First Part

Ascetical Homilies of Saint Isaac the Syrian. Trans. Dana Miller. Boston, MA: Holy Transfiguration Monastery, 1984; revised 2nd ed., 2011.

Based on both Greek and Syriac texts.

Mystic Treatises by Isaac of Nineveh. Trans. Arent Jan Wensinck. Amsterdam: Nieuwe Reeks, 1923.

Translated from Paul Bedjan's Syriac text: Amsterdam: Nieuwe Reeks, 1923. Available online at archive.org and atour.com.

On Ascetical Life: St Isaac of Nineveh. Trans. Mary T. Hansbury. New York: St Vladimir's Seminary Press, 1989.

A fresh translation of the first six discourses.

Second Part

Isaac of Nineveh: The Second Part, Chapters IV–XLI. Trans. Sebastian Brock. Leuven: Peeters, 1995.

Third Part

Isaac the Syrian's Spiritual Works. Trans. Mary T. Hansbury. Piscataway, NJ: Gorgias Press, 2016.

Primary Sources: Other Spiritual Writers

Ephrem the Syrian, Saint. *Hymns.* Trans. Kathleen E. McVey. Classics of Western Spirituality. New York: Paulist Press, 1989.

————. *Hymns on Paradise.* Trans. Sebastian Brock. Crestwood, NY: St. Vladimir's Seminary Press, 1997.

————. *The Pearl: Seven Hymns on the Faith.* Ed. John Gwynn. Trans. J. B. Morris. Saint Pachomius Orthodox Library <www .ccel.org/ccel/ephraim/pearl.i.html>.

Evagrius Ponticus: The Praktikos and Chapters on Prayer. Trans. John Eudes Bamberger. CS 5. Kalamazoo, MI: Cistercian Publications, 1972.

The Festal Menaion. Trans. Mother Mary and Kallistos Ware. London: Faber and Faber, 1969.

From Glory to Glory: Texts from Gregory of Nyssa's Mystical Writings. Trans. Colm Luibheid and Norman Russell. London: John Murray, 1962.

Gregory of Nyssa. *The Life of Moses.* Trans. Abraham J. Malherbe and Everett Ferguson. New York: Paulist Press, 1978.

John Climacus. *The Ladder of Divine Ascent.* Trans. Colm Luibheid and Norman Russell. New York: Paulist Press, 1982.

Pseudo-Dionysius. *The Complete Works.* Trans. Colm Luibheid. New York: Paulist Press, 1987.

The Wisdom of the Pearlers: An Anthology of Syriac Christian Mysticism. Trans. Brian E. Colless. CS 216. Kalamazoo, MI: Cistercian Publications, 2008.

Secondary Sources

Avis, Paul. *God and the Creative Imagination: Metaphor, Symbol and Myth in Religion and Theology.* London: Routledge, 1999.

Brock, Sebastian. *The Luminous Eye: The Spiritual World Vision of Saint Ephrem the Syrian.* CS 124. Kalamazoo, MI: Cistercian Publications, 1992.

————. *Spirituality in the Syriac Tradition.* Kottayam. St. Ephrem Ecumenical Research Institute / SEERI, 1989.

Budge, Ernest Alfred Wallis. *The Histories of Rabban Hormizd the Persian and Rabban Bar-Idta.* London: Luzac, 1902.

Campbell, Joseph. *Thou Art That: Transforming Religious Metaphor.* Novato, CA: New World Library, 2013.

Coakley, J. F. *The Church of the East and the Church of England: A History of the Archbishop of Canterbury's Assyrian Mission*. Oxford: Clarendon Press, 1992.

Cosby, N. Gordon. *By Grace Transformed: Christianity for a New Millennium*. New York: Crossroad, 1998.

Cunningham, Lawrence S., ed. *Thomas Merton, Spiritual Master: The Essential Writings*. New York: Paulist Press, 1992.

Foster, Richard. *Celebration of Discipline*. London: Harper, 1988.

Hagman, Patrik. *The Asceticism of Isaac of Nineveh*. Oxford: Oxford University Press, 2010.

Hilarion, Alfeyev. *The Spiritual World of Isaac the Syrian*. CS 175. Kalamazoo, MI: Cistercian Publications, 2000.

Hilarion, Alfeyev, ed. *St Isaac the Syrian and His Spiritual Legacy*. New York: St Vladimir's Seminary Press, 2015.

Kozeh, Mario, Abdulrahim Abu-Husayn, and Saif Shaheen Al-Murikhi, eds. *The Syriac Writers of Qatar in the Seventh Century*. Piscataway, NJ: Gorgias Press, 2014.

Lakoff, George, and Mark Johnson. *Metaphors We Live By*. Chicago: University of Chicago Press, 1980.

Leroy, Jules. *The Monks and Monasteries of the Near East*. London: Harrap & Co., 1963.

Louth, Andrew. *Denys the Areopagite*. London: Continuum, 1989.

———. *The Origins of the Christian Mystical Tradition*. Oxford: Oxford University Press, 1981.

Mary Clare, Mother. *Encountering the Depths*. London: Darton, Longman & Todd, 1981.

Matthews, Melvyn. *Both Alike to Thee: The Retrieval of the Mystical Way*. London: SPCK, 2000.

Mayes, Andrew D. *Journey to the Centre of the Soul*. Abingdon: BRF, 2017.

———. *Learning the Language of the Soul: A Spiritual Lexicon*. Collegeville MN: Liturgical Press, 2016.

Merton, Thomas. *The Asian Journal of Thomas Merton*. New York: New Directions, 1975.

Murray, Robert. *Symbols of Church and Kingdom: A Study in Early Syriac Tradition*. London: T & T Clark International, 2006.

Palmer, George E. H., Phillip Sherrard, and Kallistos Ware, trans. *The Philokalia, Volume Two*. London: Faber & Faber, 1981.

Raguin, Yves. *The Depth of God*. Wheathampstead: Anthony Clarke Books, 1975.

Ramon, Brother. *Deeper into God*. Basingstoke: Marshall Pickering, 1987.

Rohr, Richard. *Everything Belongs*. New York: Crossroad, 2003.

Scully, Jason. *Isaac of Nineveh's Ascetical Eschatology*. Oxford: Oxford University Press, 2018.

Simkins, Ronald A. *Creator and Creation: Nature in the Worldview of Ancient Israel*. Peabody, MA: Hendrickson, 1994.

Soskice, Janet M. *Metaphor and Religious Language*. Oxford: Clarendon Press, 1985.

Tillich, Paul. *The Shaking of the Foundations*. New York: Charles Scribner & Sons, 1955.

Turner, Denys. *The Darkness of God: Negativity in Christian Mysticism*. Cambridge: Cambridge University Press, 1995.

Whybrew, Hugh. *Risen with Christ*. London: SPCK, 2001.

Williams, Rowan. *The Edge of Words: God and the Habits of Language*. London: Bloomsbury, 2014.

Wren, Brian. *What Language Shall I Borrow? God-Talk in Worship*. London: SCM, 1989.